"It is clear to me as an artist that God has built be[...]
his own loveliness and creativity. We are better people w[...]
us to more exalted things, and in *Beauty Is Your Destiny*, Philip Ryken explores this
wonderful theme. It couldn't be timelier. Our culture has embraced a fascination with
ugliness. It's evident in our museums, movies, popular music, and books. I applaud
Ryken's desire to help us see how beauty reminds us that there is more—far more—to life
than a colorless, mundane 'functioning.' If your heart is hungry for vibrancy and joy,
color and meaning, then I heartily recommend this volume."

Joni Eareckson Tada, Founder and CEO, Joni and Friends International
Disability Center; author, *Joni: An Unforgettable Story* and *Songs of Suffering*

"I have been studying beauty and teaching my students about it for years. Finally,
Beauty Is Your Destiny is here, a lovely and compelling book that gathers up a treasure
trove of insights on one of the most essential qualities of our Christian faith and our
very humanity. I will return to these pages again and again and will encourage others
to do the same."

Karen Swallow Prior, author, *The Evangelical Imagination: How Stories, Images,
and Metaphors Created a Culture in Crisis*

"Philip Ryken has made a career out of studying complex truths and delivering them
to readers in accessible ways. This book about beauty stands apart from others on the
subject by way of its theological heft, biblical precision, and topical range. *Beauty Is
Your Destiny* is a gift to Christians everywhere, and I'm so glad it is in the world."

Russ Ramsey, Pastor, Christ Presbyterian Church, Nashville, Tennessee;
author, *Rembrandt Is in the Wind: Learning to Love Art through the Eyes of Faith*

"In a skeptical world of scarcity that doubts the necessity and value of biblical beauty,
Philip Ryken's work shines to illuminate 'the substance of things hoped for' and to help
us ponder the extravagance of God. As an artist, I am grateful for this book, which
affirms my path and calling to create the beautiful."

Makoto Fujimura, artist; author, *Silence and Beauty* and *Art and Faith:
A Theology of Making*

"The encouragement to 'behold' runs powerfully throughout Scripture, with some
translations using the word over 1,200 times. It's a clear exhortation to live with our
eyes wide open, and this brilliant new book from Philip Ryken is more of the same.
Every page reads like an invitation to recognize and respond to what is beautiful. We
learn that beauty may be found everywhere, from a starry night sky to a science lab to
an act of kindness—even an ancient crucifixion scene in the form of God's self-giving
love. *Beauty Is Your Destiny* is a wonderfully written book that ushers us before the glories
of our God and his world—it will no doubt lead many into worship."

Matt Redman, songwriter; worship leader

"We are made for beauty by our beautiful triune God. Therefore, we are compelled to look for beauty everywhere, even in a broken world with so much ugliness. Philip Ryken has given us a gift in *Beauty Is Your Destiny*. With masterful clarity and simplicity, he displays the variegated manifestations of beauty in this world and the sure triumph of eternal beauty through the cross of Jesus Christ."

Irwyn Ince, Coordinator, Mission to North America; author, *The Beautiful Community: Unity, Diversity, and the Church at Its Best*

"We are painfully and achingly aware of the decay and fractures to the beauty that God designed. In *Beauty Is Your Destiny*, Philip Ryken stirs the longings for beauty not simply as a keen aesthetic but as an impetus for deeper connection to God and holiness in life. Ryken reminds us that in Christ and his 'old, ugly cross,' there is a transfixing beauty—a glory worth gazing on with fresh eyes of faith and wonder—and a transforming beauty that seeks to reconcile a broken world and a broken people. This book is an ode to redemptive beauty worth relishing."

Walter Kim, President, National Association of Evangelicals

"In *Beauty Is Your Destiny*, Philip Ryken reminds us that beauty is found in God himself. Our glorious God created a world and a people to reflect his beauty. But the reality is that we live in a fallen world in which beauty is often redefined, distorted, and idolized. So God sent his beloved Son into the world as the incarnation of divine beauty. And he is transforming us into the image of his Son. One day, we will behold the Son and be like him—truly beautiful. Until then, we can make sense of the brokenness of our world and appreciate the Creator's beauty as reflected in his creation. If you want to grow in your delight of the beautiful, beginning with our beautiful God, Ryken is a trusted guide."

Juan R. Sanchez, Senior Pastor, High Pointe Baptist Church, Austin, Texas; author, *Seven Dangers Facing Your Church* and *The Leadership Formula*

"Some books on beauty are more bookish than beautiful—they engage the mind but not the heart. Ryken's *Beauty Is Your Destiny* doesn't fall into that trap. This is a book that simultaneously stimulates our minds and stirs our affections. It's informative but also pleasurable to read, leading us not only to grasp a full-orbed theology of beauty but also to worship the source from which all beauty flows."

Brett McCracken, Senior Editor, The Gospel Coalition; author, *The Wisdom Pyramid: Feeding Your Soul in a Post-Truth World*

"Philip Ryken has written a masterpiece on the subject of beauty. He has immeasurably helped us see it. Beauty is something we know, but we often fail in our attempts to describe it. Ryken depicts beauty in all its contours, showing that beauty emerges even from ugly things, such as the cross of Christ. This book combines deep and extensive knowledge with a writing style that is, well, beautiful."

William Edgar, Professor Emeritus of Apologetics, Westminster Theological Seminary

Beauty Is Your Destiny

Other Crossway Books by Philip Ryken

Beauty Is Your Destiny

How the Promise of Splendor Changes Everything

Philip Ryken

CROSSWAY®

WHEATON, ILLINOIS

Library of Congress Cataloging-in-Publication Data

Names: Ryken, Philip Graham, 1966– author.
Title: Beauty is your destiny : how the promise of splendor changes everything / Philip Ryken.
Description: Wheaton, Illinois : Crossway, 2023. | Includes bibliographical references and index.
Identifiers: LCCN 2022046449 (print) | LCCN 2022046450 (ebook) | ISBN 9781433587726 (trade paperback) | ISBN 9781433587733 (pdf) | ISBN 9781433587757 (epub)
Subjects: LCSH: Christian life. | Aesthetics—Religious aspects—Christianity.
Classification: LCC BV4501.3 .R948 2023 (print) | LCC BV4501.3 (ebook) |
    DDC 248.4—dc23/eng/20230313
LC record available at https://lccn.loc.gov/2022046449
LC ebook record available at https://lccn.loc.gov/2022046450

To Elisabeth Martha Ryken,
a child of the covenant,
with gratitude to God
for the new beauty she brings into the world

Contents

Preface

THERE IS BEAUTY ALL AROUND US. Our eyes see it in the flash of blue as a belted kingfisher dives for prey in a secluded forest pool. Our ears hear it when a soprano soars to reach the climactic notes of a love song. Our fingers feel it as we softly caress a baby's cheek. Our hearts feel it too when sworn enemies fall into a forgiving embrace. Every day we have fresh opportunities to witness the beauty of God.

The purpose of this book is to help readers both inside and outside the church become more alive to divine beauty and more aware of its place in God's plan for our lives. I hope to awaken a deeper desire for beauty that will lead to lives that are more holy, more joyful, more hopeful, and more just.

This simple yet hopefully substantive book began with a series of chapel messages at Wheaton College. That series was also titled "Beauty Is Your Destiny." It was the fall of 2021, and we were coming out of COVID (or at least we thought we were). During the pandemic I had spent more time at home and in certain respects had become more aware of God's beauty. Looking out my window every day, I saw how my garden grew. I took more long walks, which made me more attentive to the world around me. Through a season of forced isolation, I sensed a greater need for beauty—and found it.

As our students returned to campus, I wanted my chapel talks to bear witness to the beauty I had experienced. I believed that our campus community needed more beauty too. It had been a difficult time for everyone. Social distancing, mask mandates, virtual classrooms, sickness, even death—COVID-19 had taken its toll. In the United States, we had also experienced ongoing social turmoil, political polarization, and personal distress over racial injustice. Sensing our need for healing, I wanted to point our students back to God's beauty in all its dimensions.

The evangelical community has not always considered beauty a serious topic for theology or an important aspect of the Christian life. I am saddened by the story of John Muir, the Scottish American naturalist who is often regarded as the father of America's national parks. Muir was raised in a devoutly Christian home. His parents, unfortunately, did not regard his explorations in the wilderness an appropriate vocation for Christians. In fact, Muir's father pleaded with his son to abandon his "cold, icy-topped mountains" and come home "to our lovely Jesus." Not surprisingly, perhaps, Muir eventually left behind his childhood faith. Or did he? At the very same time that his father was telling him to come back to Jesus, one of his editors was telling him to stop using the word "glorious" so often to describe the American West.[1] John Muir was caught in a false dichotomy between his love for natural beauty and his impulse to praise the God of creation.

---

1   The story of John Muir's relationship with his parents is briefly related in Belden C. Lane, *Ravished by Beauty: The Surprising Legacy of Reformed Spirituality* (Oxford: Oxford University Press, 2011), 45.

Appreciating beauty—in all its splendid forms—can and should be an avenue for worship and a call to faithful Christian discipleship. Focusing on beauty also affords us an opportunity to consider a wide range of practical doctrines in fresh perspective. Over the course of this book, we consider creation and the incarnation, the Trinity and the attributes of God, the crucifixion and the resurrection, sexuality, race, justice, ecclesiology, and eschatology—all from the vantage point of sacred beauty. Indeed, one of my aims for my annual series of chapel talks is to provide a lens for Christian doctrine. Each year I try to address some of the most important topics in the Christian faith and relevant issues in contemporary life in a new and hopefully compelling way. Beauty is a worthy subject in its own right, but theological aesthetics also shows the interconnectedness of Christian doctrine.

Maybe it is important for me to say as well that this book is not just about what is beautiful; it is also about what is ugly and why. In a fallen world, any responsible discussion of the subject requires wrestling with all the ways that beauty is broken. But there is still hope. I mostly agree with Elisabeth Kübler-Ross, who claimed,

> The most beautiful people we have known are those who have known defeat, known suffering, known struggle, known loss, and have found their way out of the depths. These persons have an appreciation, a sensitivity, and an understanding of life that fills them with compassion, gentleness, and a deep loving concern. Beautiful people do not just happen.[2]

2 Elisabeth Kübler-Ross, *Death: The Final Stage of Growth* (New York: Scribner, 2009), 96.

xiii

Beautiful people do not just happen, that is true, but I want to say more. What makes us beautiful—after all our wounds and scars—is God the Holy Spirit.

Like most of my books, this one was written more out of a sense of need than out of any sense of confidence in my own expertise. Some people write what they know; I tend to write about what I want to know better. Writing about beauty makes me especially aware of my own limitations (although, admittedly, writing about topics such as the life of prayer and loving people better has been humbling too). A book about beauty should be, well, beautiful. All I can say is that I tried to write this book as beautifully as I could. You may notice that I have done a lot of quoting in its pages. Think of this book partly as a sourcebook for other Christian authors—who have written more splendidly—on the vital subject of beauty.

Thankfully, this book is much better written than it would have been without the loving labors of Andy Abernethy, Karen Lee, Dyanne Martin, Marjorie Mead, Matt Milliner, and Betsy Rockey. Each of them made invaluable improvements, both large and small. So did the editorial team at Crossway. You will have to judge whether the results are beautiful. What I know for certain is that the people who helped me write this book are beautiful, as we all should be. Beauty is our birthright and also—through Jesus Christ—our destiny.

One thing have I asked of the LORD,
   that will I seek after:
that I may dwell in the house of the LORD
   all the days of my life,
to gaze upon the beauty of the LORD.

PSALM 27:4

Lord, may we be so transformed in Your beauty that
we may be alike in beauty, and behold ourselves
in Your beauty, possessing Your very beauty.

JOHN OF THE CROSS

In the Eye of the Beholder

The Beauty of Eternity

WHERE HAVE YOU SEEN THE BEAUTY that God is bringing into the world?

I have glimpsed it in a flaming meteor streaking across the August sky and disappearing with a flash over a darkly shimmering lake. I have heard it in the laughter of a baby girl climbing up into a chair for the first time and chortling over her unexpected little triumph. I have seen it in the face of a radiant bride on her wedding day and the irrepressible tear on the cheek of her beloved groom.

I have also seen beauty rising from the ashes of a burning world. Pastor Steve Wood bore witness to such beauty as he surveyed the ruins of St. Andrew's Anglican Church in Charleston, South Carolina, in April 2018. After a long legal battle, the congregation finally had secured possession of its church building. Then disaster struck. A few hours before worship services were scheduled to begin one fine Sunday morning, fire ravaged the church. Although rescue workers salvaged the cross, the baptismal font, and the Communion table, the building was a total loss. Yet as Pastor Wood stood in the smoking ruins, he said to a reporter, "The Lord promises to bring beauty out of ashes. And we're taking Him at his word."[1]

Beauty out of ashes. The promise that Pastor Wood had in mind comes from Isaiah the prophet, who foretold a suffering Savior, anointed by the Spirit to

> provide for those who grieve in Zion—
> to bestow on them a crown of beauty
>   instead of ashes,
> the oil of joy
>   instead of mourning,
> and a garment of praise
>   instead of a spirit of despair. (Isa. 61:3 NIV)

Even when his culture was crumbling, Isaiah had the faith to see beauty rising. He knew that one day God would restore his people to their forgotten splendor.

There is beauty all around us in this grace-filled, sometimes smoldering world, if only we have the eyes to see it. There is a basis for it in the beauty of our triune God and in what he calls beautiful. There is a purpose for it too. *Beauty is our destiny.* We were born to be beautiful—to behold the beauty of our God and to be so transfixed and transformed by it that we become beautiful ourselves.

---

1   Jamie Dean recounts this true story in "Beauty out of Ashes," *World*, March 27, 2021, 38.

What Is Beauty?

My simple goal in writing this book is to awaken a longing for beauty and the eternal love of God that can be fully satisfied only in the face of Jesus Christ. My hope and prayer is that its readers will be able to look toward eternity and say, in all sincerity, what David said:

> One thing have I asked of the LORD,
>   that will I seek after:
> that I may dwell in the house of the LORD
>   all the days of my life,
> to gaze upon the beauty of the LORD
>   and to inquire in his temple. (Ps. 27:4)

Whether we know it or not, David's one desire is also our deepest longing and enduring destiny: to behold the beauty of the Lord. But as soon as we start talking about "beauty," we have difficult problems to address, starting with the conundrum of definition. What *is* beauty?

Great thinkers have wrestled with this question at least since the dawn of philosophy in ancient Greece. Today we do not seem to be much closer to an answer than we were two thousand years ago. In his book *The Beauty of the Infinite*, David Bentley Hart reluctantly concedes that it is "impossible" for anyone "to offer a definition of beauty, either in the abstract or in Christian thought."[2] Traditional definitions include concepts of beauty such as order,

---

2   David Bentley Hart, *The Beauty of the Infinite: The Aesthetics of Christian Truth* (Grand Rapids, MI: Eerdmans, 2003), 15.

proportion, symmetry, simplicity, harmony, and the pleasure they produce. Yet by themselves, these qualities do not guarantee that something is beautiful. We can all think of beautiful things that contradict the classical ideals. In fact, some of the world's most famous works of art creatively violate certain aesthetic principles. According to philosopher Roger Scruton, "Rules and precepts are there to be transcended, and because originality and the challenging of orthodoxies are fundamental to the aesthetic enterprise, an element of freedom is built into the pursuit of beauty."[3]

Even if we have trouble defining it, however, we know there is such a thing as beauty. We know this *biblically*. If we scan the pages of Scripture, we can derive a long list of things that God calls beautiful: people (Judg. 15:2; Isa. 33:17) and their melodious voices (Ezek. 33:32), animals (Jer. 13:20; 46:20), plants and trees (Dan. 4:12; Hos. 14:6), clothing (Josh. 7:21; Isa. 61:3), cities (Pss. 48:2; 50:2) and their fine buildings (Isa. 5:9), ships at sea (Isa. 2:16), and royal crowns and other treasures (Ps. 16:6; Prov. 4:9; Isa. 28:1; Ezek. 23:42).

If the Bible stipulates certain things as beautiful, then there really is beauty in the eye of the Beholder, with a capital *B*. Almighty God is inexpressibly beautiful in his own being. One early theologian thus described him as "the all-beautiful," "the superabundant source in itself of the beauty of every beautiful thing."[4] Beautiful in himself, God has also promised to "set beauty in the land of the living" (Ezek. 26:20). Whatever God sees and says is beautiful *is* beautiful! The Bible tells us so.

3 Roger Scruton, *Beauty: A Very Short Introduction* (Oxford: Oxford University Press, 2011), 119.

4 Pseudo-Dionysius, *Divine Names*, quoted in Patrick Sherry, *Spirit and Beauty: An Introduction to Theological Aesthetics*, 2nd ed. (London: SCM, 2002), 56.

We also know beauty *experientially*. In a talk titled "Why Beauty Matters," the poet Dana Gioia mentions four stages of engaging with something beautiful.[5] First, it arrests our attention; the world stops while we look or listen. Second, we have a sudden thrill of pleasure in the presence of what is truly beautiful. As the Swiss theologian Hans Urs von Balthasar testified, "Within the beautiful the whole person quivers."[6] Third, we have a sense that we are in touch with ultimate reality. Beauty is transcendent, reminding us of God. Fourth, the moment passes, and all we have left is the happy memory, which never quite matches the experience.

To Gioia's list we can add the instant desire that beauty brings to share the joy of our experience with someone else. The point is that we *all* experience beauty, and in that sense it is universal. What we see as beautiful may vary across cultures (which is yet another reason to value diversity—it helps us behold more beauty, as we see with new eyes). We also have different capacities for recognizing beauty (an aesthetic appreciation that we can develop). But beauty is more than merely a personal preference or a social construct. If God is beautiful and his creation is beautiful, then beauty is objectively there! Jonathan King summarizes by saying, "The beauty expressed in God's outward works is objectively real and subjectively experienced."[7] God has put his beauty into the world, and we are witnesses.

Our struggle to define beauty is an important signal in and of itself. Rather than giving up on beauty because it is hard for us

---

5   Dana Gioia, "Why Beauty Matters," *First Things*, February 18, 2020, https://www.first things.com/.

6   Hans Urs von Balthasar, quoted in Thomas Dubay, *The Evidential Power of Beauty: Science and Theology Meet* (San Francisco: Ignatius, 1999), 127.

7   Jonathan King, *The Beauty of the Lord: Theology as Aesthetics*, Studies in Historical and Systematic Theology (Bellingham, WA: Lexham, 2018), 50.

to agree on how to explain it, we should accept the fact that the beautiful is ineffable. In other words, beauty always goes beyond what we can describe or define, and this is an unmistakable sign of its transcendence. The overabundance of beauty in our present existence is intended to point us beyond this world to an eternal reality, "in which our immortal longings and our desire for perfection are finally answered."[8]

Beauty, Broken

We will return to beauty and eternity in a moment, but first we need to address another problem: the many ways that beauty has become broken.

In a fallen world—a world in bondage to decay (Rom. 8:21)—even the best things can become the worst. Human beings take what God made to be beautiful and turn it into something ugly. So we plunder the earth, making unsustainable demands on natural resources and devastating the visual landscape in our relentless pursuit of more. We exchange the beauty of our sexuality for the degradation of pornography. We take the ethnic diversity that ought to be one of the most beautiful things in the world—a signpost of divine creativity—and turn it into a source of damage and division. Sadly, even God's holy, beautiful church can become a place where people experience ugly abuse.

We see some of this brokenness in the world of art, where we expect instead to see rare beauty. While ugliness has its place in art that responds to a fallen world, beauty ought to have its proper place there too. Unfortunately—and although there are

8   Scruton, *Beauty*, 145.

many notable and delightful exceptions—we continue to suffer tragic loss in the visual arts, where beauty too often is dismissed, diminished, or even derided. Roger Scruton observes that

> recent art cultivates a posture of transgression, matching the ugliness of the things it portrays with an ugliness of its own. Beauty is downgraded as something too sweet, too escapist, and too far from realities to deserve our undeceived attention.[9]

One result of this contemporary attitude, writes Marilynne Robinson, is that beauty "as a conscious element of experience, as a thing to be valued and explored, has gone into abeyance among us."[10] Even if these complaints are overstated and the tide is beginning to turn,[11] surely we can agree with Scruton and Robinson that there is not as much beauty in the contemporary art world as there could be or ought to be.

We also struggle with our own desire for beauty. This too is broken. Not that wanting to be beautiful is wrong in itself. If beauty is our destiny, then our desire to be beautiful is divinely ordained. Yet our perceptions are problematic—both of our own beauty and of the beauty of others. We focus on what is merely external rather than on what is truly and intrinsically beautiful. Too often we see ourselves as a distorted image. Then we find ourselves asking the haunting question that Bono asks in "City

---

9   Scruton, *Beauty*, 140.
10 Marilynne Robinson, "Story, Culture, and the Common Good," *Breaking Ground*, October 16, 2020, https://breakingground.us.
11 See, for example, Matthew J. Milliner, "Makoto Fujimura and the Art of New Creation," *Marginalia*, May 6, 2022, https://themarginaliareview.com/.

of Blinding Lights": "What happened to the beauty I had inside of me?"[12]

Consider, as one example of broken beauty, the anxiety many people experienced when the world moved online at the start of the global COVID-19 pandemic. Students and workers had to look at themselves on the screen all day long. Under their own critical gaze, many struggled with the reality gap between the way they looked and the way they wanted people to see them.

The constant barrage of images of so-called beauty on social and visual media only makes matters worse. So do beauty products, beauty salons, beauty pageants, and almost anything else that begins with "beauty." It is unsettling to know that many film stars dread being recognized in public because they do not look as good in person as they do in the movies. If celebrities struggle with body shame, then what hope is there for the rest of us? In her widely read essay on the damaging effects of cultural attitudes about physical beauty, especially for women of color, sociologist Tressie McMillan Cottom closes with this haunting line: "Ugly is everything done to you in the name of beauty."[13]

Sadly, someday whatever beauty we *do* have will be lost—this too is a problem! As the aging process accelerates, our bodies become less beautiful, and with our inevitable demise will come the loss of our ability to witness the world's beauty. Nothing seemed more futile to the French existentialist philosopher Simone de Beauvoir than the end of beauty that death would bring. She

---

12 U2, "City of Blinding Lights," compact disc, track 5 on *How to Dismantle an Atomic Bomb*, Interscope Records, 2004.

13 Tressie McMillan Cottom, *Thick and Other Essays* (New York: The New Press, 2019), 72.

wrote, "I think with sadness of all the books I've read, all the places I've seen, all the knowledge I've amassed and that will be no more. All the music, all the paintings, all the culture, so many places: and suddenly nothing."[14] The melancholy chorus in Johannes Brahms's setting of Nänie—a poem by Friedrich Schiller—puts us in a similar mood. "Even beauty must perish," the choir sings, "and all the perfect must die."[15]

Dust we are, and to dust we will return. How then will beauty rise from these mortal ashes?

The Beatific Vision

It helps us if we see how the story ends. In Psalm 27, when King David expressed his one and only heart's desire, he was looking forward to an enduring beauty. The king said that he wanted to gaze at God all the days of his life. He longed for what theologians call "the beatific vision"—the blissful visual experience of beholding the very face of God. "The Beatifical Vision," wrote the brilliant Puritan theologian John Owen, is such a "sight of God and his Glory, especially as manifested in Christ, as will make us *blessed* unto eternity."[16]

We can see some of God's beauty now, as we explore throughout this little book. In coming chapters, we consider the beauty that God has for us in himself, in his fair creation, in the people he made in his image, in the church (of all places), in culture and

---

14 Simone de Beauvoir, *Force of Circumstance*, quoted in Dubay, *Evidential Power of Beauty*, 99.

15 Johannes Brahms, *Nänie*, funeral song for orchestra and mixed chorus, musical setting of a poem by Friedrich Schiller (Leipzig: C. F. Peters, 1881). Public domain.

16 John Owen, *Christologia*, quoted in Hans Boersma, *Seeing God: The Beatific Vision in Christian Tradition* (Grand Rapids, MI: Eerdmans, 2018), 322.

the arts, and most of all in the life-giving sacrifice of his beautiful Son, who in time will make us gloriously beautiful as well. Yet the beauty we see now is only a glimpse of the surpassing beauty that we will experience forever in the life to come—what the Bible calls "the light of the knowledge of the glory of God in the face of Jesus Christ" (2 Cor. 4:6).

Too many Christians are unaware of this thrilling biblical promise or else have neglected to consider its implications for Christian discipleship. But here is the gospel truth: if we are children of God through faith in the suffering death and bodily resurrection of Jesus Christ, then our destiny is to gaze on his enthralling beauty forever.

"Now we see in a mirror dimly," the Scripture says, "but then face to face" (1 Cor. 13:12). There are hints of this promise throughout Scripture. When Moses came down from Mount Sinai, for example, his face was unbearably radiant, for he had been in God's very presence (Ex. 34:29–35). When Job was in despair, he consoled himself with this assurance:

> I know that my Redeemer lives,
>> and at the last he will stand upon the earth.
> And after my skin has been thus destroyed,
>> yet in my flesh I shall see God. (Job 19:25–26)

When Peter, James, and John ascended the Mount of Transfiguration, they saw the resplendent glory of God radiating from the face of Jesus Christ (Luke 9:28–36). When we read all the way to the end of the story, we learn that the saints who live forever in Christ's glorious presence "will see his face" (Rev. 22:4).

Throughout church history, our fathers and mothers in the faith lived in the hope that they would see the beautiful face of God. Irenaeus said, "For the glory of God is a living man; and the life of man consists in beholding God."[17] "Every face has beauty," wrote Nicholas of Cusa, "but none is beauty itself. Your face, Lord, . . . is absolute beauty itself, which is the form that gives being to every form of beauty. O immeasurably lovely Face."[18] On her dying day, Teresa of Avila told the loved ones at her bedside that it was time for her to move on. Then she addressed her Savior directly: "O my Lord and my Spouse, the hour that I have longed for has come. It is time for us to see one another."[19] The same hope motivated the five missionaries who participated in Operation Auca and were martyred in the Amazonian jungle. Afterward, Olive Fleming bore witness to the hope she held for her husband, Pete, who was one of the martyrs: "Pete had one great desire in life. His one desire was to see Christ. Now he sees Him, and therefore I'm happy, because I know that Pete's one desire has been fulfilled."[20] There is also Dante Alighieri, of course, whose entire *Divine Comedy* is a quest to experience the beatific vision. Dante wrote, "O plenitude of grace, by which I could presume to fix my eyes upon eternal Light until my sight was spent on it!"[21]

17 Irenaeus, *Against Heresies*, quoted in King, *Beauty of the Lord*, 110.
18 Nicholas of Cusa, *De visione Dei*, quoted in Boersma, *Seeing God*, 397.
19 Teresa of Avila, quoted in "Did You Know? Nuns, Prophets, Queens, Witches, Wives," *Christian History* 131, 2019, 1.
20 Olive Fleming, in the audio recording of a 1956 talk by David Howard, the brother of Elisabeth Elliot, whose husband Jim also participated in Operation Auca and was one of the five martyrs; shared by the courtesy of Janet Howard.
21 Dante, *Paradiso*, trans. Jean Hollander and Robert Hollander, ed. Robert Hollander (New York: Doubleday, 2007), 33.82.

Or consider the thrilling invitation that the Puritan Thomas Watson gave his congregation in London, England:

> Imagine what a blessed sight it will be to see Christ wearing the Robe of our human nature, and to see that nature sitting in glory above the Angels. If God be so beautiful here in his Ordinances, Word, Prayer, Sacraments, if there be such excellency in him when we see him by the eye of faith through the prospective glass of promise, O what will it be when we shall see him *face to face!* . . . There will be glory beyond *Hyperbole*; if the Sun were ten thousand times brighter than it is, it could not so much as shadow out this glory; in the heavenly Horizon we shall behold beauty in its first magnitude and highest elevation; there we shall *see the King in his glory* [Isa. 33:17]. All lights are but Eclipses, compared with that glorious Vision.[22]

Many New England Puritans expressed a similar hope by carving a striking image into their gravestones: the outline of a simple face with lidless eyes. This image expressed their gospel anticipation that in the resurrection they would look on the lovely face of Jesus Christ with unblinking gaze.

Both the promise of Scripture and the consistent record of Christian history bear witness that beauty is our destiny. This beauty is not just in the eye of the Beholder, notes the artist Bruce Herman; it is also in the face of our Beloved![23]

22 Thomas Watson, *The Beatitudes: or, A Discourse upon Part of Christs Famous Sermon on the Mount* (London, 1660), 336.

23 Bruce Herman, "Wounds and Beauty," in *The Beauty of God: Theology and the Arts*, ed. Daniel J. Treier, Mark Husbands, and Roger Lundin (Downers Grove, IL: IVP Academic, 2007), 118.

We Become What We See

On the day we see this beauty for ourselves, something amazing will happen to us: we ourselves will become gloriously beautiful. The Bible promises a marvelous transformation, in which we *become* the beauty we have always longed for. The beatific vision, wrote John Owen, is "perfectly and absolutely *transforming*. It doth change us wholly into the Image of Christ."[24]

The basis for this miraculous change is the beauty of Jesus Christ, the Son of God, who is "the radiance of the glory of God and the exact imprint of his nature" (Heb. 1:3). To see the face of our risen Redeemer truly is to behold the glory of God, for as Jesus himself said, "Whoever has seen me has seen the Father" (John 14:9).

When we see our Savior's divine glory with our own two eyes, its resplendence will so illuminate us that we will radiate with the glory of God. In short, seeing is becoming! To see Jesus is to become beautiful—as he is. We know this from David's declaration: "Those who look to him are radiant" (Ps. 34:5). We also know it from the promise of the apostle John: "Beloved, we are God's children now, and what we will be has not yet appeared; but we know that when he appears we shall be like him, because we shall see him as he is" (1 John 3:2). When John says that we will be like Jesus, he means that when our physical bodies are raised to resurrection life, then we too will "bear the image of the man of heaven" (1 Cor. 15:49) and will shine like the sun (see Matt. 13:43), in moral and physical perfection. We are waiting for "the redemption of our bodies"

---

24 Owen, *Meditations and Discourses on the Glory of Christ*, quoted in Boersma, *Seeing God*, 324.

(Rom. 8:23), when by the power of the Holy Spirit, the Lord Jesus "will transform our lowly bod[ies] to be like his glorious body" (Phil. 3:21; cf. 1 Cor. 6:14). We really were born to be beautiful!

When theologians throughout church history have contemplated the beatific vision, they have considered not only what we will behold but also what we will become. To behold the beauty of the Lord is to enter ever more completely and gloriously into the light of our Savior. As we gaze at him in wonder, he looks back at us with love. This face-to-face encounter causes an interchange of glory, which Jonathan Edwards described as "both the *emanation* and the *remanation*. The refulgence shines upon and into the creature and is reflected back to the luminary."[25] As a result of this interchange, we are changed from the inside out. Edwards again:

> The pleasure of seeing God is so great and strong that it takes the full possession of the heart; it fills it brimful, so that there shall be no room for any sorrow, no room in any corner for anything of an adverse nature from joy. There is no darkness can bear such powerful light. It is impossible that they that see God face to face, that behold his glory and love so immediately as they do in heaven, should have any such thing as grief or pain in their hearts.[26]

The Puritan Isaac Ambrose compared our face-to-face encounter with Jesus Christ to the long, adoring looks that lovers share:

25 Jonathan Edwards, *Dissertation concerning the End for Which God Created the World*, quoted in Owen Strachan and Douglas Sweeney, *Jonathan Edwards on Beauty*, Essential Edwards Collection (Chicago: Moody Publishers, 2010), 17.

26 Edwards, "Pure in Heart Blessed," in Boersma, *Seeing God*, 366–67.

They look, and gaze, and dart their beams: and reflect their glories on each other. Oh the communications! Oh the darting of beams betwixt Christ and his Saints! Look as when two admirable persons, two lovers meet together, their eyes sparkle, they look on, as if they would look through one another. And such is the effect of these looks.[27]

When as believers who live in the eye of the Beholder we gaze on the face of our Beloved, we will become beautiful beyond anything we could ever imagine.

Based on the promises of the Bible, the beautification of believers in glory is instantaneous; it happens the moment we behold the risen Christ. But it also appears to be eternally progressive. As beautiful as we will become when we finally see Jesus face-to-face, we will become even *more* beautiful in the infinite ages to come, when "we all, with unveiled face," will be "transformed into the same image from one degree of glory to another" (2 Cor. 3:18).

Seeing God's Beauty

What difference does it make to know that beauty is our destiny?

As believers in a beautiful Savior, we should have a heightened awareness of the beauty of creation, of the brokenness of beauty in a fallen world, and of the beauty God is bringing in our redemption. The world is more beautiful for us and also more painful. But we are not without hope because by his beautiful life and death and resurrection, Jesus has the power to bring beauty out of ashes. "In Jesus Christ," writes Jeremy Begbie, "divine beauty

---

27 Isaac Ambrose, *Looking unto Jesus*, quoted in Boersma, *Seeing God*, 318.

has, so to speak, got to grips with the wounded and deformed beauty of the world; in the incarnate Son, crucified, risen and now exalted, we witness God's re-creation of the world's beauty."[28]

Redemptive beauty is for now as well as later. Even as we await our final beautification, we catch present glimpses of God's redeeming beauty. These previews of the beatific vision give us rising hope that one day we will see the face of God.

As president of Wheaton College, I see God's beauty on our campus every day. I see it in ardent student worship. I see it when summer turns to fall and the trees show the colors from their autumn collection. I see it in the love that caregivers in our Community School of the Arts show to children with special needs as they share the gift of music. I see it too when roommates have a conflict and then reconcile.

I also see beauty across the subjects we study in our Christ-centered liberal arts curriculum. It is in the Scriptures of the Old and New Testaments, in all their literary variety. It is in cultures and communities and in the mysteries of the human heart and soul. It is in the beauty of words—how they are written and spoken in English and other languages. It is also in the austere beauty of numbers and equations. Edna St. Vincent Millay rightly declared, in the title to one of her poems, "Euclid Alone Has Looked on Beauty Bare."[29]

Scientists also see beauty everywhere as they study the natural world. To give just one example, a team of lab physicists thrilled

---

28 Jeremy S. Begbie, "Created Beauty: The Witness of J. S. Bach," in Treier, Husbands, and Lundin, *Beauty of God*, 27.

29 Edna St. Vincent Millay, "Euclid Alone Has Looked on Beauty Bare," Poetry Foundation, accessed December 19, 2022, https://www.poetryfoundation.org/.

the world in 2021 by exposing the inner workings of the aurora borealis, or northern lights. Working in UCLA's plasma labs under the leadership of Jim Schroeder, these scientists demonstrated for the first time that when electrons shooting out from solar winds collide with earth's upper atmosphere, they surf electromagnetic Alfvén waves to reach speeds up to forty million miles per hour, thus producing the spectacular colors of the polar lights.[30] This discovery adds more wonder and awe to our experience of beauty, as science often does. When we keep our eyes wide open, we see the beauty of God everywhere we look, from earth to sky.

Pure Beauty

Our loving Lord gives us these varied glimpses of intrinsic beauty to awaken in us a transcendent, expectant desire that will be fully and finally satisfied when we gaze into the face of Jesus Christ. In the meantime, seeing the grandeur that God brings everywhere into the world helps us "live in eternity's sunrise," as the poet William Blake once expressed it.[31] Such experiences awaken our aesthetic appreciation, sharpen our spiritual sensibilities, and produce in us a deep longing to go beyond these earthly glimpses and get to the place where we can gaze.

The Bible makes it clear that "no one has ever seen God" (John 1:18), "who dwells in unapproachable light" (1 Tim. 6:16), because no sinful mortal can behold the glory of God's unmediated holiness—and then live to tell about it (Ex. 33:20). But the Bible

---

30 Tiara Walters, "Making Heaven in a Lab: Scientists Solve the Mystery of the Aurora," *Daily Maverick*, June 12–18, 2021, 168.

31 William Blake, "Eternity," Academy of American Poets, accessed December 19, 2022, https://www.poets.org/. Public domain.

also promises that one day we will see God's glory for ourselves, in the face of our beautiful Savior.

I will never forget the moment when my daughter Kathryn was baptized. Since we are faithful Presbyterians, this was infant baptism, and I was holding my baby girl in my arms. The minister reminded us that the name Kathryn comes from the Greek word for pure. Then he quoted a blessed promise that includes her precious name—a promise Jesus gave in his Sermon on the Mount: "Blessed are the pure in heart, for they shall see God" (Matt. 5:8). The whole spinning world stopped in that moment as I looked down into the face of my beautiful Kathryn—blessed and pure—and knew how her story would end: one day *my* beloved would look into *her* Beloved's face.

This promise is for all God's pure ones—his precious sons and daughters. If you are a child of God, made pure by the righteous blood of your Savior, then beauty is your destiny too—the eternal, shining beauty you will behold and become forever when you see your crucified, risen Lord Jesus face-to-face.

Your eyes will behold the king in his beauty.

ISAIAH 33:17

The pinnacle of beauty, the beauty toward which all creatures point, is God. He is supreme being, supreme truth, supreme goodness, and also the apex of unchanging beauty.

HERMAN BAVINCK

2

The King in His Beauty

The Beauty of the Trinity

EVERY GENERATION HAS AT LEAST ONE big question it wants to get answered before it will believe in God—a question Christians need to address in gospel perspective if we want to win people to faith in Christ.

In a 2021 talk he gave for the National Association of Evangelicals, James Choung looked back over the last seventy-five years and concluded that baby boomers—born between the end of World War II and the rise of the Civil Rights Movement—want to know *what is true*. To share the gospel with them, we need to do classic apologetics and give them reasons to believe. Generation Xers are suspicious of hypocrisy and inauthenticity; they want to know *what is real*. Millennials, born at the end of the twentieth century, want to know *what is good*. They will follow Christ only if they can see that the church is righteous. So what about digital natives, the iGen?

Choung contends that the current generation wants to know *what is beautiful*.[1]

To be sure, nearly everyone asks all these questions sooner or later. Philosophers have been debating the good, the true, and the beautiful since the days when Plato strolled around Athens with Socrates. We all wonder why there is something rather than nothing. But at this moment in history—when we are assaulted everywhere by the ugliness of transgression—we have a deep longing for what is truly beautiful. It is not enough anymore to tell people that the gospel is true or even that it works; they need to see for themselves that it is beautiful.

Visible Beauty

If we ask the question "What is beautiful?" perhaps the first thing we notice is the beauty of the world around us, including the beauty of humanity. But the most basic beauty is the one true God. He is "beauty itself, the source of beauty in all other things."[2] His divine being is "the Beauty behind every beauty,"[3] the basis for every other beautiful thing. Nothing is beautiful apart from God.

The theologian who saw this truth most clearly may have been Jonathan Edwards, who said more about God's beauty than any theologian before and maybe since. God alone is "infinitely the

---

1 James Choung, who serves as vice president of strategy and innovation for InterVarsity Christian Fellowship, gave this talk to board members of the National Association of Evangelicals on March 3, 2021.

2 Patrick Sherry, *Spirit and Beauty: An Introduction to Theological Aesthetics*, 2nd ed. (London: SCM, 2002), 53.

3 Steve DeWitt, *Eyes Wide Open: Enjoying God in Everything* (Grand Rapids, MI: Credo, 2011), 7.

most beautiful," Edwards wrote, "and all the beauty to be found throughout the whole creation is but the reflection of the diffused beams of that Being who hath an infinite fullness of brightness and glory; God is . . . the foundation and fountain of all being and all beauty."[4] Elsewhere, Edwards highlighted the beauty of God by drawing a series of comparisons:

> The beauty of trees, plants, and flowers, with which God has bespangled the face of the earth, is delightful; the beautiful frame of the body of man, especially in its perfection, is astonishing; the beauty of the moon and stars is wonderful; the beauty of highest heavens is transcendent; the excellency of angels and the saints in light is very glorious: but it is all deformity and darkness in comparison of the brighter glories and beauties of the Creator of all. . . . The very angels, they hide their faces before him.[5]

It is doubtful whether anyone ever had a deeper longing for this divine beauty than King David. As we saw in the previous chapter, David's sole desire was to behold "the beauty of the LORD"—not just to glimpse it but to gaze upon it (Ps. 27:4). Israel's king expressed the same desire at the end of one of his other psalms. Looking ahead to the rising of a bright new day—and perhaps to the dawn of eternity—he testified,

---

4 Jonathan Edwards, *The Nature of True Virtue*, quoted in DeWitt, *Eyes Wide Open*, 18.
5 Jonathan Edwards, "God's Excellencies," quoted in Owen Strachan and Douglas Sweeney, *Jonathan Edwards on Beauty*, Essential Edwards Collection (Chicago: Moody Publishers, 2010), 30.

As for me, I shall behold your face in righteousness;
> when I awake, I shall be satisfied with your likeness. (Ps.
> 17:15)

David's singular desire to see God's face tells us many important things about beauty. It tells us that beauty is real. It tells us that there is a basis for beauty in the being of God. It tells us that God's beauty is deeply satisfying. And it tells us that his divine beauty is something we can see for ourselves. Our goal in this chapter is precisely that: to see God as beautiful—visibly, invisibly, triunely beautiful.

God's beauty is, first of all, *visible*. One of the reasons we know that God wants us to see his beauty is because scattered throughout the Scriptures are stories of people who beheld the glory of God, which is a visible manifestation of his beauty. Moses saw this, for example, when he went up on Mount Sinai and was surrounded by the glory of God like a consuming fire (Ex. 24:15–18), and again when God's glory passed close by him (Ex. 33:18–22) and he beheld the beauty of God's goodness and grace. The children of Israel saw it when the glory of God fell on the tabernacle and that holy structure became so resplendent that no one could enter (Ex. 40:34–35). Isaiah saw it when he went into the temple and saw the Lord on his glorious throne, high and lifted up, in the adoration of holy angels (Isa. 6:1–3). The disciples saw it too when they climbed the Mount of Transfiguration and Jesus appeared to them in his true divine glory (Matt. 17:1–3).

The Bible tells us these stories to convince us that God is beautiful and also to give us the hope that one day we will see his beauty for ourselves. What Moses, what Isaiah, what Peter, James, and John witnessed were preappearances of the beatific vision that every believer will see one day in the face of Jesus Christ.

Notice the word that these Bible stories use to describe the beauty of God: not *beauty* but *glory*. Beauty and glory are closely related, virtually synonymous. The Russian theologian Sergei Bulgakov proclaimed, "God is glorious, and His Glory is beauty itself."[6] The glory of God—his radiant appearance in unbearable light—is the outward manifestation of his inner beauty, or what Jonathan Edwards called his "lovely majesty."[7] A more recent theologian clarifies the correspondence between beauty and glory by defining the glory of God as "the supereminently luminous beauty of divinity beyond all experience and all descriptions, all categories, a beauty before which all earthly splendors, marvelous as they are, pale into insignificance."[8]

To see God's beauty in the Bible, therefore, we need to do more than simply look for the word *beautiful*; we must include the passages that speak of *glory*, *splendor*, and *majesty*.[9] As the psalmist declares,

Splendor and majesty are before him;
strength and beauty are in his sanctuary. (Ps. 96:6;
cf. 145:5)

6 Sergei Bulgakov, "Religion and Art," quoted in Sherry, *Spirit and Beauty*, 5.

7 Jonathan Edwards, *A Treatise concerning Religious Affections*, quoted in Sherry, *Spirit and Beauty*, 12.

8 Thomas Dubay, *The Evidential Power of Beauty: Science and Theology Meet* (San Francisco: Ignatius, 1999), 45. For a careful delineation of the differences between divine beauty and divine glory, see Jonathan King, *The Beauty of the Lord: Theology as Aesthetics*, Studies in Historical and Systematic Theology (Bellingham, WA: Lexham, 2018), 44–52.

9 For a complete list of beauty-related terms in the Bible, see King, *Beauty of the Lord*, 338–39.

Invisible Beauty

The reason why God sometimes makes himself visibly glorious is so we know that beauty is one of his essential attributes. Although we often leave it off the list, God's infinite beauty belongs alongside infinite wisdom, infinite power, and infinite love as one of his defining characteristics. Indeed, Edwards believed that God is "distinguished from all other beings, and exalted above them, chiefly by his divine beauty."[10]

If beauty is one of God's eternal divine attributes, then he has inner as well as outer beauty. What a fortunate few have seen outwardly when they beheld the glory of God is present constantly within his very being. God's beauty is invisible as well as visible, and the two are inseparably connected: God's visible beauty helps us perceive what is unseen.

Theologians throughout Christian history have emphasized the inner divine beauty of Jesus Christ. Our hope is that one day we will see the glory of God (literally!) in the face of Jesus Christ. But even that beatific vision will be more than skin deep; it will also be a spiritual perception. The glorified saints in heaven, wrote Jonathan Edwards,

> will behold an outward glory as they [behold] the human nature of Christ, which is united to the Godhead, as it is the body of that person that is God. And there will doubtless be appearances of a divine and inimitable glory and beauty in Christ's glorified body, which it will indeed be a ravishing and blessed

10 Jonathan Edwards, *A Treatise concerning Religious Affections*, quoted in Belden C. Lane, *Ravished by Beauty: The Surprising Legacy of Reformed Spirituality* (Oxford: Oxford University Press, 2011), 173.

sight to see. But the beauty of Christ's body that will be beheld with bodily eyes will be ravishing and delighting chiefly as it will express his spiritual glories. The majesty that will appear in Christ's body will express and show forth the spiritual greatness and majesty of the divine nature. The pureness and beauty of that light and glory will express the perfection of divine holiness. The sweetness and ravishing mildness of his countenance will express his divine and spiritual love and grace.[11]

Similarly, the Dutch theologian Abraham Kuyper argued that our "direct seeing" of the risen Lord Jesus Christ "with the bodily eye" will be accompanied with "a spiritual vision" of his divine beauty.[12] We will see within Christ's outward, incarnate, resurrected appearance to comprehend the beautiful essence of his inward divine nature with our minds and hearts. The visible will be a portal to the invisible.

Thankfully, we do not have to wait for that beatific vision to see the beauty of God. By faith we may contemplate the beauty in the other divine attributes revealed in sacred Scripture. There is beauty in the love God shows to people who are lost and forgotten. There is beauty in his grace for penitent sinners—the grace that the poet Gerard Manley Hopkins referred to as God's "better beauty."[13] There is beauty in the kindness God shows in taking care of us every day and providing everything we truly need.

11 Edwards, "Pure in Heart Blessed," quoted in Hans Boersma, *Seeing God: The Beatific Vision in Christian Tradition* (Grand Rapids, MI: Eerdmans, 2018), 367.

12 Abraham Kuyper, *Diktaten Dogmatiek*, quoted in Boersma, *Seeing God*, 346.

13 Gerard Manley Hopkins, "To What Serves Mortal Beauty?," quoted in Sherry, *Spirit and Beauty*, 33.

There is beauty in his justice; he will right every wrong. There is also beauty in our Savior's humility—in the way he stoops to our level so that we can know him and love him.

The list goes on. There is also beauty in God's goodness and truth. For Hans Urs von Balthasar, beauty "dances as an uncontainable splendor around the double constellation of the true and the good."[14] There is a reason why the good, the true, and the beautiful have always been at the core of Christian thought: it is because they are united in the character of God and incarnate in the person of his Son. The prophet Zechariah conjoined these attributes when he exclaimed, "How great is his goodness, and how great is his beauty" (Zech. 9:17).

To summarize, beyond simply being a divine attribute in its own right, beauty is an aspect of *all* God's attributes. Some theologians categorize beauty as one of God's "transcendental properties"—in other words, it is an essential quality of the divine nature that inheres in each and every one of his individual attributes.[15] We see this perhaps most clearly in God's holiness—in the way he is set apart from everyone and everything else in absolute purity. When the prophet Isaiah beheld the divine King "high and lifted up" in the temple of God, the angels declared him the thrice-holy God (Isa. 6:1–3). Like the rest of God's attributes, his holiness too is beautiful. Thus, Edwards was so captivated by the holiness of God that he regarded it as deeply

14 Hans Urs von Balthasar, *The Glory of the Lord: A Theological Aesthetics*, vol. 1, *Seeing the Form*, quoted in Lisa Coutras, *Tolkien's Theology of Beauty: Majesty, Splendor, and Transcendence in Middle-Earth* (London: Palgrave Macmillan, 2016), 14.

15 Stratford Caldecott, *Beauty for Truth's Sake: On the Re-enchantment of Education* (Grand Rapids, MI: Brazos, 2009), 31.

attractive, despite his own unrighteousness. "Holiness," he said, is "the infinite beauty and excellence" of God.[16] It *is* "in a peculiar manner the beauty of the divine nature."[17]

Anyone who has ever come close to the holiness of God has found it utterly, beautifully breathtaking. It is because of this holy beauty that the angels in God's sanctuary forever cry out to one another,

Holy, holy, holy is the LORD of hosts;
the whole earth is full of his glory. (Isa. 6:3)

What is true of God's holiness is true of every divine attribute: the more we behold its beauty, the more we are drawn into the heartfelt adoration of God. Beauty is the attribute of God "through which we are able to view the majesty of all his other perfections."[18] Perhaps we could go further and stipulate that God *is* beauty itself. In any case, whether beauty is synonymous with God or whether we regard it as a separate attribute or as a quality of all his attributes—the beauty of God leads us to the highest praise.

Beautiful Trinity

Our sense of God's holy beauty, whether visible or invisible, gets multiplied when we perceive it as triune. There is one God in three persons—the Father, Son, and Holy Spirit—whom John Donne

---

16 Jonathan Edwards, *Essay on the Trinity*, quoted in Sherry, *Spirit and Beauty*, 13.

17 Edwards, *A Treatise concerning Religious Affections*, quoted in Sherry, *Spirit and Beauty*, 33.

18 Irwyn Ince, *The Beautiful Community: Unity, Diversity, and the Church at Its Best* (Downers Grove, IL: InterVarsity Press, 2020), 28.

acclaimed in one of his sonnets as the "three person'd God."[19] In this eternal mystery, we behold "a community of diversity bound together in unity."[20] This "triunity of God," claimed Karl Barth, "is the secret of God's beauty."[21] Each person of the Trinity is uniquely and individually beautiful. This beauty, however, gets expanded exponentially within the mysterious interplay of intra-Trinitarian relationships. There is a triunity of beauty within the Godhead as the Father images his beauty in his only begotten Son and as the Father and the Son together emanate the beautiful Spirit, who in turn glorifies both the first and second persons of the Trinity.

The Father is beautiful—beautiful in his mighty power, steadfast faithfulness, and loving grace for his wayward children. He is beautiful like the father in the story of the prodigal son, who ran to meet his rebellious, long-lost son and wrapped him in his loving arms (Luke 15:20). He is the protective Father of widows and orphans (Ps. 68:5), the gentle Father of kindness (Eph. 2:7), and the merciful Father of all compassion (2 Cor. 1:3). He is the God whom Peter praised as "the Majestic Glory" (2 Pet. 1:17). When Augustine considered his deep need for the loving fatherhood of God, he cried out, "O my supreme and good Father, Beauty of all things beautiful."[22]

The Father is beautiful too in his love for his beloved Son—the one he did not spare but gave up freely for us all (Rom. 8:32). That Son, in turn, is as beautiful in his own being as the Father is.

19 John Donne, "Holy Sonnet 14: Batter My Heart" (1633), in *John Donne's Poetry: Authoritative Texts, Criticism*, ed. A. L. Clements, Norton Critical Edition (New York: Norton, 1963), 86.

20 Lane, *Ravished by Beauty*, 164.

21 Karl Barth, *Church Dogmatics*, 2.1:651, quoted in Lane, *Ravished by Beauty*, 159.

22 Augustine, *Confessions*, quoted in Sherry, *Spirit and Beauty*, 8.

In fact, the Son came for the very purpose of showing us the Father's beauty. God the Son came into the world so that we could see what Isaac Ambrose called "the substantial reflection of the Father's light and glory in Jesus Christ."[23] "We have seen his glory," the Scripture proclaims, "glory as of the only Son from the Father" (John 1:14; cf. Luke 2:32).

In his perfect life, healing miracles, kingdom gospel, obedient surrender, suffering cross, atoning sacrifice, luminous resurrection, and resplendent ascension, Jesus shows us the beauty of God. He shows us this beauty in his physical body—the body in which, one day, we will see "displayed the loveliness of the Godhead."[24] The beatific vision will reveal to our own eyes the most beautiful sight we have ever beheld, for it is only "in the risen and ascended Christ" that "creation's beauty has reached its culmination."[25]

There is still more to be said, however, because the Spirit also is beautiful. In his famous poem "God's Grandeur," Gerard Manley Hopkins declared that the world is "charged with the grandeur of God," which will "flame out, like shining from shook foil." Hopkins closed by imagining the Holy Spirit as the one who "over the bent / World broods with warm breast and with ah! bright wings."[26] This was the poet's way of saying that the Holy Spirit gives the world its grandeur, its beauty. We should also bear in mind that everything we read in the Bible was breathed out by the Holy Spirit

---

23 Isaac Ambrose, *Looking unto Jesus*, quoted in Boersma, *Seeing God*, 318.

24 Strachan and Sweeney, *Jonathan Edwards on Beauty*, 74.

25 Jeremy S. Begbie, "Created Beauty: The Witness of J. S. Bach," in *The Beauty of God: Theology and the Arts*, ed. Daniel J. Treier, Mark Husbands, and Roger Lundin (Downers Grove, IL: IVP Academic, 2007), 27.

26 Gerard Manley Hopkins, "God's Grandeur" (1877), in *God's Grandeur: The Poems of Gerard Manley Hopkins* (McLean, VA: Trinity Forum, 2016), 24. Public domain.

(2 Tim. 3:16), including everything the Scriptures say about the beauty of the Father and the Son. From this sacred fact—the Spirit's glorious revelation of the Father and the Son—we may deduce that the Holy Spirit loves to make things beautiful.[27]

If the Spirit is the beautifier of the Father by inscripturating his beauty, the Spirit is also the beautifier of the Son by raising him from the dead in his glorious resurrection body. The Spirit is also the beautifier of creation because—with the Father and the Son—the Spirit made everything there is and made it very good. The Spirit is the beautifier of the church—the one who works in us to make us beautiful like Jesus. In short, the Holy Spirit is the Beautiful Spirit. When the Bible says that God "has made everything beautiful in its time" (Eccl. 3:11), therefore, it is testifying most directly to the work of God's Spirit. As Jonathan Edwards said, "It was made especially the Spirit's work to bring the world to its beauty."[28]

How to See God's Beauty

Now the same Holy Spirit wants to do something beautiful for us: help us see the beauty of God—the visible, invisible, and triune beauty of God. How does the Spirit do this?

To begin with, the Holy Spirit helps us experience God's beauty in creation. As we will consider more closely in the following chapter, the natural world puts many of God's beautiful attributes on public display. According to Romans, everyone ought to be able to see this, but the only people who truly recognize it are filled with God's Spirit. The merely natural mind does not and

27 This is the main thesis of Patrick Sherry's helpful book *Spirit and Beauty*.
28 Jonathan Edwards, *Miscellanies*, quoted in Sherry, *Spirit and Beauty*, 86.

cannot discern the truth of God from creation (see Rom. 1:19–21; cf. 8:5–10). Without the Holy Spirit, people see only creation's beauty but not beauty's Creator.

The Spirit also helps us see God's beauty in the Bible, where we behold his beauty on every page. The place where we learn specifically about God's invisible and triune beauty is in the Scriptures of the Old and New Testaments. As we encounter the Bible's saving message, we are captivated by the loveliness of the Father, the Son, and the Holy Spirit. Meditating on God's holy, inspired word gives us a daily experience of divine beauty.

Finally, the Holy Spirit helps us see God's beauty through prayer. When we pray, the Spirit of God helps us cry out to our heavenly Father with our soul's deep longings (Rom. 8:26) and then works in the world to advance the kingdom of God. The more we pray, the more we see God at work: wounds are healed, relationships are reconciled, sins are forgiven, and souls are set free. Wherever God is at work, everything becomes more beautiful. By praying in the Spirit, therefore, we are empowered to perceive the beauty of his saving and sanctifying work in the answers to our prayers.

Don't Miss Out!

Until we see this beauty for ourselves, we are missing out on what matters most. This was Augustine's lament when he finally came to faith in Christ after wasting years of his life through spiritual neglect. With sadness, the great theologian confessed,

> I took too long to fall in love with you, beauty so ancient and so new. I took too long to fall in love with you! But there you were, inside, and I was outside—and there I searched for you,

and into those shapely things you made, my misshapen self went sliding. You were with me, but I wasn't with you. Those things, which wouldn't exist unless they existed in you, held me back, far from you. You called and shouted and shattered my deafness. You flashed, you shone, and you put my blindness to flight. You smelled sweet, and I drew breath, and now I pant for you. I tasted you, and now I'm starving and parched; you touched me and I burst into flame with desire for your peace.[29]

Augustine was filled with holy regret that he waited so long to see God's beauty. If we are wise, we will refuse to make the same mistake. Rather than delaying a moment longer, we will fall in love with the one true and beautiful God.

The reason why this generation (really, every generation) wants to know what is beautiful is because God created us with a deep longing for beauty that only he can satisfy. Whenever we feel dissatisfied (as we often do), whenever we feel lonely or unhappy, whenever we have longings in life that go unfulfilled—this should be a sign for us of our deep need for God. Whether he realized it or not, the poet Oscar Wilde was expressing this divine longing when he wrote, "Man is hungry for beauty. There is a void."[30] When we trace our own hungry disappointments back to our deepest desire, we discover that the only thing big enough to fill the void is the beauty of God the Father, God the Son, and God the Holy Spirit.

---

29 Augustine, *Confessions: A New Translation*, trans. Sarah Ruden (New York: Modern Library, 2017), 312–13 (10.38).

30 Oscar Wilde, quoted in Richard Ellman, "Wilde in New York: Beauty Packed Them In," *New York Times* (November 1, 1987).

The reason why King David was so desperate to see God was because he knew that God alone could satisfy his soul. Consider again the closing words of Psalm 17:

As for me, I shall behold your face in righteousness;
    when I awake, I shall be satisfied with your likeness.
        (Ps. 17:15)

Until we see God's true beauty, we will miss the real beauty in everything else. That is why a chapter on the beauty of God needs to come near the beginning of this book: it is the foundation for everything that follows. Without God, we will never experience the beauty of creation, which is made for his praise. We will never experience the true beauty of humanity, which is made in his image. We will never understand the beauty of sexual purity the way that God designed it. We will never experience the beauty of beloved community, which comes only as a gift of God's Spirit. We will never see the beauty of justice either; we will simply replace one form of oppression with another.

When we do see the beauty of God, we see the absolute beauty in everything else as a reflection of his divine glory. Then our souls are satisfied! One glimpse of God's beauty "can sweep the heart upward," writes Robert O'Connell, "to Himself, to the swelling fountain of unfailing sweetness that alone can satiate the soul's deep thirst for beauty."[31]

---

31 Robert O'Connell, *Art and the Christian Intelligence in St. Augustine*, quoted in James Fodor, "The Beauty of the Word Re-membered: Scripture Reading as a Cognitive/Aesthetic Practice," in Treier, Husbands, and Lundin, *Beauty of God*, 165.

Something important—indeed, necessary—happens whenever we find ourselves in the presence of something that is truly beautiful: everything stops. Beauty arrests our attention. Rather than quickly moving on to the next thing, we linger in the presence of what we know is beautiful.

Therefore, if we find it hard to linger in God's presence—hard to pray, hard to worship, hard to meditate on God's word—then we must not be seeing the true beauty of the triune God because when we do see the beauty of the Father, Son, and Holy Spirit, then all we want to do is stay with him.

Whenever seeing God's beauty in this way is a personal struggle—as it is for all of us sometimes—it will help us pray these words from the Book of Common Prayer: "O God, . . . mercifully grant that we, being delivered from the disquietude of this world, may by faith behold the King in his beauty."[32] This is a prayer we know God will answer because the Bible gives us this sure and certain promise: "Your eyes *will* behold the king in his beauty" (Isa. 33:17).

32 *Book of Common Prayer*, "Collect for the Transfiguration" (New York: Church Publishing, 1979), 191.

The heavens declare the glory of God,
and the sky above proclaims his handiwork.

PSALM 19:1

God's activity as Creator infuses the realm of creation
with a beauty derived from his own Being.

LISA COUTRAS

3

For the Beauty of the Earth

The Beauty of Creation

IN AUGUST 2017, researchers with the Laser Interferometer Gravitational-Wave Observatory (LIGO) detected and observed for the first time the collision of two massive neutron stars. The waves emanating from the collision were followed seconds later by a fiery flash of gamma radiation. When the scientists analyzed their scans of the resulting debris, they concluded that the explosion had produced 236 sextillion tons of pure gold, which is forty times the mass of our entire world.[1]

If we could venture far enough into outer space, where there are two hundred billion stars in each of two hundred billion galaxies, we could gather the gold dust wherever those four hundred billion trillion stars collide. Truly, the heavens are telling the glories of God!

---

1 Priyamvada Natarajan, "All Things Great and Small," *New York Review of Books*, July 1, 2021, 58.

If we pay attention, we can also behold the beauty much closer to home. In his "Personal Narrative," the theologian Jonathan Edwards described walking in the pastures near his boyhood home in rural Connecticut. "As I was walking there," Edwards wrote, looking up at the sky and clouds, "there came into my mind a sweet sense of the glorious majesty and grace of God, that I know not how to express."[2] Yet try to express it he did. Edwards later testified,

> I often used to sit and view the moon, for a long time; and so in the daytime, spent much time in viewing the clouds and sky, to behold the sweet glory of God in these things: in the meantime, singing forth with a low voice, my contemplations of the Creator and Redeemer.[3]

From that time forward, Edwards tells us,

> my sense of divine things gradually increased, and became more and more lively, and had more of that inward sweetness. The appearance of everything was altered: there seemed to be, as it were, a calm, sweet cast, or appearance of divine glory, in almost everything. God's excellency, his wisdom, purity, and love, seemed to appear in everything: in the sun, moon, and stars; in the clouds, and blue sky; in the grass, flowers, trees; in the water, and all nature.[4]

---

2   Jonathan Edwards, "Personal Narrative," quoted in Owen Strachan and Douglas Sweeney, *Jonathan Edwards on Beauty*, Essential Edwards Collection (Chicago: Moody Publishers, 2010), 47–48.

3   Edwards, "Personal Narrative," quoted in Strachan and Sweeney, *Jonathan Edwards on Beauty*, 52.

4   Jonathan Edwards, quoted in Steve DeWitt, *Eyes Wide Open: Enjoying God in Everything* (Grand Rapids, MI: Credo, 2011), 121.

For anyone who has eyes to see—anyone who is freed from the bondage and blindness of sin to perceive the Creator of creation—this world is filled with the glory of God. The primary purpose of this chapter is to give us eyes to see, so that our daily experience of life in this beautiful world gives us the same wonder that it gave Edwards—and produces as much praise.

The Heavens Are Telling

The beauty of the earth and the God who made it is the first main theme of Psalm 19, which C. S. Lewis called "the greatest poem in the Psalter and one of the greatest lyrics in the world."[5] King David begins with a bold assertion:

> The heavens declare the glory of God,
>> and the sky above proclaims his handiwork. (Ps. 19:1)

In other words, the natural world bears witness to divine beauty. Creation gives testimony to its Creator. Or maybe we should say instead that through his creation, our Creator gives testimony to himself. God "has made everything beautiful in its time," says Ecclesiastes 3:11, and in this way he displays his own eternal beauty.

King David amplifies his point by describing several characteristics of creation's testimony. It is *articulate*; it speaks to us clearly. Notice carefully the vocabulary that the psalmist uses to describe creation's voice—both the nouns and the verbs:

> The heavens declare the glory of God,
>> and the sky above proclaims his handiwork.

---

5 C. S. Lewis, *Reflections on the Psalms* (New York: Harcourt, Brace & World, 1958), 63.

Day to day pours out speech,
    and night to night reveals knowledge.
There is no speech, nor are there words,
    whose voice is not heard.
Their voice goes out through all the earth,
    and their words to the end of the world. (Ps. 19:1–4b)

Declare, proclaim, reveal—those are the verbs. The nouns are *speech, words,* and *voice.* Each of these terms describes something clearly communicated and plainly understood. Whatever creation is telling us, it is something that we are well able to understand. The Netherlands Confession of Faith thus compares creation to a form of literature: the world is set "before our eyes as a beautiful book, in which all created things, great and small, are like letters, which give us the invisible things of God to behold, namely His eternal power and divinity."[6]

John Calvin said something similar. The great theologian loved to go to Lake Geneva by night and gaze at the stars, which he aptly described as "the alphabet of theology."[7] Creation is a "book written in large enough letters," Calvin also said, to read the knowledge of God.[8] Or consider the testimony of the Puritan Richard Baxter, who loved his evening rambles through the

---

6   Netherlands Confession of Faith, quoted in E. John Walford, "The Case for a Broken Beauty: An Art Historical Viewpoint," in *The Beauty of God: Theology and the Arts*, ed. Daniel J. Treier, Mark Husbands, and Roger Lundin (Downers Grove, IL: IVP Academic, 2007), 97.

7   John Calvin, *Commentary on the Psalms*, quoted in Belden C. Lane, *Ravished by Beauty: The Surprising Legacy of Reformed Spirituality* (Oxford: Oxford University Press, 2011), 74.

8   Calvin, *Psalms*, quoted in Lane, *Ravished by Beauty*, 59.

English Midlands: "What an excellent book is the visible world for the daily study of a holy soul!"[9]

Creation's testimony—so articulate—is also *incessant*. According to Psalm 19:2, the world has a good deal to say about the glory of God. The speeches it gives on the subject "pour out." Day after day and night after night, the heavens and the earth refuse to be silent. When it comes to their Creator, they will and must be loquacious.

To give one notable example, simply look at the sun, which testifies always and everywhere to the glory of God. The psalmist compares its ascent to a groom who can hardly wait to meet his bride and to a long-distance runner in peak physical condition who finishes the race that he starts:

> In [the heavens] he has set a tent for the sun,
>> which comes out like a bridegroom leaving his chamber,
>> and, like a strong man, runs its course with joy.
> Its rising is from the end of the heavens,
>> and its circuit to the end of them,
>> and there is nothing hidden from its heat. (Ps. 19:4c–6)

The sun is only one of creation's witnesses to the radiant glory of God. Everything in creation stands as a constant testimony to its Creator. Here is John Muir, exploring the great American West, describing a scene he witnessed near the Columbia River: "The whole mountain appeared as one glorious manifestation of divine power, enthusiastic and benevolent, glowing like a countenance

---

9   Richard Baxter, *The Christian Directory*, quoted in Lane, *Ravished by Beauty*, 109.

with ineffable repose and beauty before which we could only gaze in devout and lowly admiration."[10]

This incessant, articulate testimony is also *universal*—as universal as the rising and setting sun. Wherever we go in the world, creation has something to say. As the psalmist puts it,

> There is no speech, nor are there words,
>> whose voice is not heard.
> Their voice goes out through all the earth,
>> and their words to the end of the world. (Ps. 19:3–4b)

Because its language is universal, people of every tribe and tongue can understand what creation is saying. We hear it from the sun and moon, the rugged mountains and starry midnight lakes, the fruit trees and flower beds. The Puritan Ralph Austen—who wrote a marvelous treatise on the spiritual lessons he learned from walking in his orchard—believed that the very trees "always speak Rationally and Religiously; in everything taking God's part, speaking of his praise and glory; and for the instruction of all men."[11]

Theater of God's Beauty

What specifically are the heavens trying to tell us? This articulate vocabulary, this incessant speech, this universal language—what is it saying?

One good place to answer this question is the first chapter of Paul's letter to the Romans, which claims that God has plainly

---

10 John Muir, quoted in DeWitt, *Eyes Wide Open*, 79.

11 Ralph Austen, *A Dialogue (or Familiar Discourse) and Conference between the Husband-man and Fruit Trees*, quoted in Lane, *Ravished by Beauty*, 35.

shown us what we can know about his divine being. All over the world, Paul says, God's "invisible attributes, namely, his eternal power and divine nature, have been clearly perceived, ever since the creation of the world, in the things that have been made" (Rom. 1:20).

Apart from omnipotence, the apostle declines to list the specific divine attributes that are revealed through creation. But theologians have taken their cue from this verse and named many character traits that God has revealed in creating this universe: infinite knowledge, sustaining providence, matchless wisdom, intrinsic goodness, and so on. Writing late in the fifteenth century, the Renaissance humanist Marsilio Ficino concluded, "By its utility, harmony, and decorativeness, the world testifies to the skill of the divine artist and is proof that God is indeed its Maker."[12] When the Puritan Thomas Taylor considered the world's abundant variety of plants and animals, he said, "Here be millions of Ministers and Apostles sent by God into the world, to preach unto men the inexhaustible treasures of their Lord's goodness, wisdom, and power."[13] "All creatures have a teaching voice," wrote another Puritan, Joseph Caryl; "they read us divinity Lectures of Divine Providence."[14]

Taylor and Caryl may have been taking their cue from John Calvin, who believed similarly that "all creatures, from those in the heavens to those under the earth, are able to act as witnesses and messengers of God's glory." Then Calvin proceeded to give

---

12 Marsilio Ficino, quoted in Patrick Sherry, *Spirit and Beauty: An Introduction to Theological Aesthetics*, 2nd ed. (London: SCM, 2002), 3.

13 Thomas Taylor, *Meditations from the Creatures*, quoted in Lane, *Ravished by Beauty*, viii.

14 Joseph Caryl, *An Exposition upon the Book of Job*, quoted in Lane, *Ravished by Beauty*, 116.

examples: "For the little birds that sing, sing of God; the beasts clamor for him; the elements dread him, the mountains echo him, the fountains and flowing waters cast their glances at him, and the grass and the flowers laugh before him."[15] Calvin continued by explaining what we learn from the messages of these living apostles:

> We see, indeed, the world with our eyes, we tread the earth with our feet, we touch innumerable kinds of God's works with our hands, we inhale a sweet and pleasant fragrance from herbs and flowers, we enjoy boundless benefits; but in those very things of which we attain some knowledge, there dwells such an immensity of divine power, goodness, and wisdom, as absorbs all our senses.[16]

More than anything else—even more than power and wisdom—what creation reveals to us is God's infinite beauty. Surely a beautiful world could come only from a beautiful God. Indeed, the created world participates in its Creator's beauty. So Augustine exclaimed, when surveying the wonders of creation, "It was You, Lord, who made them: for you are beautiful and they are beautiful!"[17] This beauty derived from Beauty is specifically triune, as "out of their shared love, the Father and Son breathe forth the Holy Spirit as Beautifier, restlessly extending their beauty beyond themselves to everything in creation."[18]

---

15 John Calvin, *Commentaries*, quoted in W. David O. Taylor, *The Theater of God's Glory: Calvin, Creation, and the Liturgical Arts* (Grand Rapids, MI: Eerdmans, 2017), 44.

16 John Calvin, *Commentary on Genesis*, quoted in Taylor, *Theater*, 34.

17 Augustine, *Confessions*, quoted in Sherry, *Spirit and Beauty*, 8.

18 Lane, *Ravished by Beauty*, 164.

When speaking about the beauty of God extended throughout creation, it is easy to keep quoting from the church's great
theologians, who reserved some of their highest praises and most
beautiful phrases for this subject. In one of his favorite analogies,
John Calvin referred to the visible universe as "the theater of God's
glory." Every human being, he wrote, is "formed to be a spectator of
the created world and given eyes that he might be led to its author
by contemplating so beautiful a representation."[19] Creation thus
stands as a dramatic witness to the existence of God. "As soon as we
acknowledge God to be the supreme Architect," Calvin also said,
"who has erected the beauteous fabric of the universe, our minds
must necessarily be ravished with wonder at his infinite goodness,
wisdom, and power."[20] God has created us to behold his beauty,
which his beautiful Spirit reveals everywhere in the world around
us. John Newton's observation of the natural world inspired him
to declare in one of his many pastoral letters that God "adorns
the insects and the flowers of the field with a beauty and elegance
beyond all that can be found in the courts of kings."[21] Jonathan
Edwards was similarly effusive in describing the wonders of the
natural world as "emanations of the sweet benevolence of Jesus
Christ" and "shadows of his infinite beauties and loveliness."[22]

When the Reverend Maltbie Davenport Babcock went out walking in upstate New York, he would tell Mrs. Babcock that he was
"going out to see the Father's world." This became the inspiration
for a well-known Christian hymn. "This is my Father's world," sings

19 John Calvin, *Commentary on Romans*, quoted in Lane, *Ravished by Beauty*, 58.
20 John Calvin, *Psalms*, quoted in Lane, *Ravished by Beauty*, 69.
21 John Newton, *Select Letters of John Newton* (Edinburgh: Banner of Truth, 1960), 163.
22 Jonathan Edwards, *Miscellanies*, quoted in Sherry, *Spirit and Beauty*, 14.

one of Babcock's middle stanzas; "he shines in all that's fair."[23] The whole world is indeed shining with the radiant beauty of God.

Beauty is one of the primary love languages of our wonder-working God. Decades ago, students at one of the country's most secular art schools—Philadelphia's University of the Arts—invited me to start a Bible study in the central cafeteria. We decided to start at Genesis 1:1 and discuss everything the Bible had to say about God as artist—the original, cosmic artist. By the time we came to the end of the school year, we were still talking about the opening chapters of Genesis because the story of creation has so much to say about the artistry of our Creator.

Some of the strongest testimonies to the beauty of creation come from what scientists say about the role of beauty in confirming their discoveries. Although we often associate beauty with the arts, it is equally important in science and mathematics. One survey of the history of science argued that beauty is a primary criterion for scientific truth and concluded that the elegance of most equations is as strong a proof for their validity as an empirical experiment. For example, after James Watson and Francis Crick first theorized the double helix structure of human DNA, they went to lunch excitedly telling one another that "a structure this pretty just had to exist."[24]

The compelling beauty of science has led many scientists to trust in Christ. To give just one example, the world-renowned astronomer David Block was elected as a fellow of the Royal Astronomical Society of London when he was only nineteen years

---

23 Maltbie Davenport Babcock, "This Is My Father's World" (1901). Public domain.

24 Thomas Dubay relates this anecdote in *The Evidential Power of Beauty: Science and Theology Meet* (San Francisco: Ignatius, 1999), 114.

old. Block was so moved by what he witnessed in the heavens that one day he turned to his mentor and said, "The universe is so beautiful, both visually and mathematically!"[25] The recognition of this fact was the start of a spiritual journey that led the young scientist to personal faith in Jesus Christ.

Seeing Beauty

As David Block's testimony demonstrates, our witness to creation always demands a personal response. This beauty that we see all around us—how should we respond? And what is our responsibility as a result?

First, *attention*: attend to creation. Beauty is designed to stop us in our tracks. God has put his splendor into the world so that we will set aside everything else for the moment and behold his wonders. The psalmist said,

> On the glorious splendor of your majesty,
> and on your wondrous works, I will meditate. (Ps. 145:5)

Wise Christians have always been intentional about slowing down and taking time to enjoy the world around them. Augustine exhorted, "Some people read books in order to find God. But the very appearance of God's creation is a great book. Look above you! Look below you! Take note! Read!"[26]

A marvelous example of looking above and below is the C. S. Lewis scholar Clyde S. Kilby, who made a series of personal

---

25 David Block, "What the Heavens Declared to a Young Astronomer," *Christianity Today*, March 2021, 87.

26 Augustine, quoted in Taylor, *Theater*, 60.

resolutions, or daily principles he purposed to live by. The first was this: "At least once every day I shall look steadily up at the sky and remember that I, a consciousness with a conscience, am on a planet traveling in space with wonderfully mysterious things above me and about me." Dr. Kilby's sixth resolution is similarly attentive to the wonders of creation:

> I shall open my eyes and ears. Once every day I shall simply stare at a tree, a flower, a cloud, or a person. I shall not then be concerned at all to ask *what* they are but simply be glad that they are. I shall joyfully allow them the mystery of what Lewis calls their "divine, magical, terrifying and ecstatic" existence.[27]

Adoring Beauty

Second, Kilby's resolutions invite us to do more than notice the world around us: we should enjoy it! Another good example to follow is the English essayist, biographer, and lay theologian G. K. Chesterton, who wrote in one of his letters, "I do not think there is anyone who takes quite such a fierce pleasure in things being themselves as I do. The startling wetness of water excites and intoxicates me: the fieriness of fire, the steeliness of steel, the unutterable muddiness of mud."[28]

Even if we are not all called to be scientists, all of us can become—like Chesterton and Kilby—amateur naturalists who are easily arrested by the beauty of creation and attend to its daily

---

27 Clyde S. Kilby, "A Means to Mental Health," Marion E. Wade Center, 2011, accessed July 5, 2022, https://www.wheaton.edu/. For more on Kilby, see "Clyde S. Kilby," Marion E. Wade Center, accessed July 5, 2022, https://www.wheaton.edu/.

28 G. K. Chesterton, quoted in Dubay, *Evidential Power of Beauty*, 175–76.

splendors. This will not only increase our enjoyment of everyday life, but it will also lead us to praise our Maker. It was said of Saint Francis of Assisi: "In beautiful things he saw Beauty itself and through his vestiges imprinted on creation he followed his Beloved everywhere."[29]

Like Francis, we too should follow beauty to its ultimate source and turn our attention into *adoration*. This is what David does in Psalm 19: he lets creation's pleasures lead him to praise. When the king says, "The heavens declare the glory of God," he is not simply describing something; he is celebrating it. This is what the Bible does whenever it talks about the beauties of creation. God is to be honored, God is to be praised, God is to be worshiped for the worlds he has made. Jonathan Edwards rightly said, "God is glorified not only by His glory's being seen, but by its being rejoiced in."[30]

Sometimes atheists and other skeptics talk about the difficult questions they demand to have answered before they will believe in God, such as the so-called problem of evil. These hard questions do deserve good answers. But unbelievers also have some challenges of their own that they need to face, and one of them is the problem of wonder. Everyone can see the beauty in this world, even when it is broken. Such beauty surely requires a beautifier. Yet when skeptics see the world's beauty, they have no one to thank for it and no one to praise. How frustrating it must be to receive the gift of beauty and yet be unable to acknowledge it properly.

29 Bonaventure, *The Life of Saint Francis*, quoted in James Fodor, "The Beauty of the Word Re-membered: Scripture Reading as a Cognitive/Aesthetic Practice," in Treier, Husbands, Lundin, *Beauty of God*, 173n30.

30 Jonathan Edwards, *Miscellanies*, quoted in Lane, *Ravished by Beauty*, 175.

One of our everyday privileges as believers in Christ is knowing whom to worship. C. S. Lewis once said that in the experience of enjoying the world's beauty, he tried "to make every pleasure into a channel of adoration."[31] John Piper took Lewis's channel and widened it:

> We don't just stand outside and analyze the natural world as a beam [of sunlight], but let the beam fall on the eyes of our heart, so that we see the source of the beauty—the original beauty, God himself. . . . All of God's creation becomes a beam to be "looked along" or a sound to be "heard along" or a fragrance to be "smelled along" or a flavor to be "tasted along" or a touch to be "felt along." All our senses become partners with the eyes of the heart in perceiving the glory of God through the physical world.[32]

Anyone can perceive God's glory in creation—not just scientists and theologians. A notable example comes from Abigail Adams, the second first lady of the United States.[33] On a trip across the Atlantic Ocean—in the calm that followed a turbulent storm—Adams witnessed the stunning beauty of the bioluminescent sea creatures that surrounded the ship for miles in every direction. As she looked out in ecstatic wonder on a phosphorescent ocean, she found herself quietly murmuring these words of praise: "Great

---

31 C. S. Lewis, *Letters to Malcom: Chiefly on Prayer* (New York: Harcourt, 1992), 89.

32 John Piper, *When I Don't Desire God: How to Fight for Joy* (Wheaton, IL: Crossway, 2004), 184–85.

33 This story is recounted briefly in David McCullough, *John Adams* (New York: Simon & Schuster, 2001), 295.

and marvelous are thy works, Lord God Almighty; in wisdom hast thou made them all" (cf. Ps. 104:24).

Keeping Beauty

There is a third response we should have to the beauty of this natural world: attention, adoration, and *protection*. As Christians we have a duty to care for the beauty that God has placed under our dominion. "Our task as a species," writes Belden Lane, is to "identify and honor the conjoining . . . of the speechless splendor of creation, bringing everything to its fullness in the glory of God."[34]

Never in the history of the world has creation care been a more urgent priority for the people of God than it is at the present moment, when human beings have such a massive influence on the natural world. As a result of our actions and inactions, many parts of the world are becoming increasingly inhospitable. We see the consequences of our fallen condition in the accelerated scarcity of resources and surge in natural disasters. But we are also suffering a tragic loss of beauty: the melting of glaciers, the bleaching of coral reefs, the destruction of rainforests, the silencing of songbirds. Lane calls this "spiraling loss" what it is: "not only an ecological crisis, but also a failure of human beings to celebrate what God has made," which in turn "diminishes our capacity to show forth the luster of the Holy Trinity."[35]

Such concern for creation is not uniquely pagan but deeply Christian. And it is nothing new. The best theologians have *always* regarded our God-given dominion over creation as a stewardship

34 Lane, *Ravished by Beauty*, 195.
35 Lane, *Ravished by Beauty*, 160.

of loving care.[36] From William Wilberforce—who was nearly as concerned about the mistreatment of animals as he was about the abolition of slavery—to Jonathan Edwards—who frankly regarded such abuse as a perversion of the purposes of God—thoughtful Christians have long sought to protect the creatures that the Lord has given into our watchful care.[37] And they have done so for profoundly theological reasons. Listen to Calvin's logic: "If now I seek to despoil the land of what God has given it to sustain human beings, then I am seeking as much as I can to do away with God's goodness."[38]

Of course, it is true that God has promised to make new heavens and a new earth. Although the world was "subjected to futility" because of humanity's sin, this was done in the hope that it would be "set free from its bondage to corruption" and "obtain the freedom of the glory of the children of God" (Rom. 8:20–21). The Creator has promised that one day creation itself will be redeemed and restored by the risen Lord Jesus Christ. More specifically, creation will be gloriously transformed by the risen Christ through the power of the Holy Spirit. The Russian Orthodox theologian Sergei Bulgakov beautifully encapsulated this unbreakable promise: "The whole world, too, the waters and the land, will be transfigured by the Holy Ghost, and will appear in their beauty."[39]

In the meantime, however, *this* heavens and *this* earth—the ones that King David declared are telling us the glory of God—

---

36 Perhaps the best historical overview of Christian reflection on creation care is Fred Van Dyke, *Between Heaven and Earth: Christian Perspectives on Environmental Protection* (Santa Barbara, CA: Praeger, 2010).

37 Lane, *Ravished by Beauty*, 191.

38 John Calvin, *Sermons on Deuteronomy*, quoted in Lane, *Ravished by Beauty*, 29.

39 Sergei Bulgakov, quoted in Sherry, *Spirit and Beauty*, 5.

are the only heavens and the only earth we have. We are called, therefore, to protect them until Jesus comes again. We may not be the guardians of the galaxy, but at least we can become protectors of the planet by fighting to save what we love.

We carry out this calling in the hope that others will join us in seeing the world's beauties and then lifting praise to the God who made them. Beauty also has a role to play in reaching the lost. Our heart's desire—as we attend, adore, and protect—is for creation to do what it was designed to do and lead people to see the beauty of Jesus Christ as Creator and Redeemer. Then they will join us in giving the strong, clear personal testimony that the Puritan poet Elizabeth Rowe gave when she declared, "The God of nature, and the original of all beauty, is my God."[40]

---

40 Elizabeth Rowe, *Devout Exercises of the Heart*, quoted in Lane, *Ravished by Beauty*, 17.

I praise you, for I am fearfully and wonderfully made.
Wonderful are your works;
*   my soul knows it very well.*

PSALM 139:14

Where we place beauty on our list of priorities reflects
what we understand about what beauty means in
being human. The ability to appreciate it and cultivate
it reflects our nature as beings made in the image
of God, the creator of and source of all beauty.

KAREN SWALLOW PRIOR

4

You Are So Beautiful

The Beauty of God's Image

THE SPARKLING NEW MEYER SCIENCE CENTER on the campus of Wheaton College was almost complete. The state-of-the-art facility featured new classrooms and instructional laboratories, permanent spaces for faculty and students to collaborate on scientific research, a magnificent observatory for stargazing, and a new home for the massive skeleton of a prehistoric mastodon.

As the dean of natural and social sciences, Dorothy Chappell had designed large, colorful murals to tell the story of each scientific discipline: biology, chemistry, physics, and so on. Yet as I surveyed the plans, I realized that something was missing. I also knew where to find it. So I reached out to my mother-in-law—Elaine Arison Maxwell, class of 1951—to ask if she would consider contributing the missing piece to the science center. It was the bronze sculpture in Elaine's living room, first cast by the artist Kirsten Kokkin for the baptistry at a church in Norway. The sculpture depicted a baby boy resting in two large hands and bore the evocative title "In God's Hands."

When this sculpture was installed, the Meyer Science Center finally had its most important occupant. Until that moment, the exhibits revealed everything in God's beautiful creation from the rocks to the stars, including the iconic Perry Mastodon. But the building did not yet have a display to represent the greatest masterpiece in the world: a human being.

Body Beautiful

Human beings have been created from the overflow of beauty in the Father, the Son, and the Holy Spirit. There are many wonders in the universe, but *we* are the fairest of them all! Nothing in all creation is more magnificent than persons made in the sacred image and likeness of God. We alone have a beauty beyond anything else that God has ever made.

When King David celebrated the beauty of humanity in Psalm 139, he wrote with unmistakable wonder for the gift of his physical body:

> For you formed my inward parts;
>> you knitted me together in my mother's womb.
> I praise you, for I am fearfully and wonderfully made.
> Wonderful are your works;
>> my soul knows it very well.
> My frame was not hidden from you,
> when I was being made in secret,
>> intricately woven in the depths of the earth.
>> (Ps. 139:13–15)

Here David is talking about his conception and gestation. He knew that his life was more than the mere product of a sexual and biological process. He was handcrafted by the Creator, who knows everything about him and made him just the way he is. What was true of King David is true for every one of us: even if no one was there to witness it, our parts were put together by the intricate wisdom of our wonder-working God. "We have been made by the ultimate artisan," writes Sam Allberry. "Our God has produced millions of human bodies, but we are not mass-produced."[1] Therefore, each of us is unique.

Elsewhere, David declared that human beings are made only "a little lower than the heavenly beings / and crowned with glory and honor," with "dominion over the works" of God's hands (Ps. 8:5–6). Most English translations say "glory," but they might as well say "beauty." We are crowned with *beauty*, and thus we have a unique place in the universe. To say that we are a little lower than the angels is to say that we are the highest creatures on earth. As sons and daughters of the Most High God, we are princes and princesses of his coming kingdom.

Our unique status was first announced at the beginning of the world. On the sixth day of creation, the triune God said, "Let us make man in our image, after our likeness" (Gen. 1:26). This declaration gets underscored by repetition and expanded to make it clear that the image of God inheres equally in both sexes:

So God created man in his own image,
in the image of God he created him;
male and female he created them. (Gen. 1:27)

---

1 Sam Allberry, *What God Has to Say about Our Bodies: How the Gospel Is Good News for Our Physical Selves* (Wheaton, IL: Crossway, 2021), 25.

Here we have the bedrock theological principle of *imago Dei*, the image of God. We alone in all creation are made to bear the likeness of God—in beauty, authority, and intimacy. In his celebrated sermon "The American Dream," Martin Luther King Jr. explained the implications of our creation in the image of God:

> The whole concept of the *imago Dei* . . . is the idea that all men have something within them that God injected. Not that they have substantial unity with God, but that every man has a capacity to have fellowship with God. And this gives him a uniqueness, it gives him worth, it gives him dignity. And we must never forget this as a nation: there are no gradations in the image of God. Every man from a treble white to a bass black is significant on God's keyboard, precisely because every man is made in the image of God. One day we will learn that. We will know one day that God made us to live together as brothers and to respect the dignity and worth of every man.[2]

Our unique status as image bearers helps explain why the universe seems to have been made with our existence in mind. This is true individually. King David describes God's purpose:

> Your eyes saw my unformed substance;
> in your book were written, every one of them,
>> the days that were formed for me,
>> when as yet there was none of them. (Ps. 139:16)

---

2   Martin Luther King Jr., "The American Dream," quoted in Irwyn Ince, *The Beautiful Community: Unity, Diversity, and the Church at Its Best* (Downers Grove, IL: InterVarsity Press, 2020), 50–51.

What was true for David personally is true for humanity universally: even before we were formed, God had a place and a plan for us. "The human fit with the biosphere is so precise," argues Michael Denton, "that the design must have been built into the universe."[3] Human beings are the culmination of creation. In recent decades, many physicists and astronomers—whether they are Christians or not—have concluded that from the very first millisecond when it exploded into being, the universe developed in amazingly precise ways that not only accommodated but almost seemed to require human existence. Cosmologists call this "the fine-tuned universe" or the "anthropic principle."[4] Human beings are the focus of creation.

When God made us to be his unique image bearers, with a special place in his universe, he decided to make us beautiful. This is true visibly: there is beauty in our physical form. The Bible openly declares that specific people are beautiful in their outward appearance, such as Sarai (Gen. 12:11, 14), Moses (Acts 7:20; Heb. 11:23), David (1 Sam. 16:12), Abigail (1 Sam. 25:3), and Esther (Est. 2:7; cf. Gen. 29:17; Job 42:15)—not to mention the unforgettable bride in the Song of Songs, who was "beautiful as the moon, bright as the sun" (Song 6:10; cf. 1:15; 2:10; 4:1; 5:9). This beauty inheres equally in both men and women. Male and female, our bodies display "a fit, a mutual enhancement, a beautiful difference, at the heart of what God has made."[5] It is also

---

3　Michael Denton, as quoted in Thomas Dubay, *The Evidential Power of Beauty: Science and Theology Meet* (San Francisco: Ignatius, 1999), 184.

4　Dubay, *Evidential Power of Beauty*, 212.

5　Andrew Wilson, "Beautiful Difference: The (Whole-Bible) Complementarity of Male and Female," The Gospel Coalition, May 20, 2021, https://www.thegospelcoalition .org/.

true universally: there is something beautiful in people of every ethnicity and every physicality, of every color, shape, and size.

We should be careful, therefore, not to have too limited a view of humanity's physical beauty. In an article titled "Who Gets to Judge What's Beautiful?," Robin Givhan rightly advocates for a "new outlook on beauty" that "doesn't ask us to come to the table without judgment" but does ask us "to come presuming that everyone in attendance has a right to be there."[6] There is beauty in *every* human body. Too often, we use the word *beautiful* to describe certain people, whom we distinguish from people we think are *average looking* or even *homely*. But we are *all* fearfully and wonderfully made, and God made each of us just the way he wanted us to be. We are called, therefore, to look at one another with what Esther Lightcap Meek calls "the generous, self-giving gaze, the noticing regard of another person."[7]

We are also called to receive our own bodies with gratitude. Sooner or later, all of us encounter features we do not particularly like about our physical form, but we should remember to be grateful for all the things we *do* like. Although we all have frustrations and limitations with our physical form, we also have blessings and opportunities. God made us just the way we are, and aspects of beauty are evident in every one of us—what Edward Farley calls "the inevitable grace of a living body."[8] To give just one example of our magnificent design, consider what goes on inside our heads. Accord-

---

6 Robin Givhan, quoted in Susan Goldberg, "Who Gets to Judge What's Beautiful?," *National Geographic*, January 2020, 6.

7 Esther Lightcap Meek, quoted in the front matter to Ince, *Beautiful Community*.

8 Edward Farley, *Faith and Beauty: A Theological Aesthetic* (2001; repr., New York: Routledge, 2016), 98.

ing to one description, "The brain weighs less than three pounds, yet a computer capable of handling a single brain's output would cover the entire earth. The brain sorts one hundred million bits of data from the eyes, nose and other sensory outposts each second, yet uses far less electricity than the average lightbulb."[9] Amazing!

King David would not be surprised to learn of such wonders. When he celebrated how awesomely he was made, he was not considering himself to be a special case but was relishing the magnificence in every one of us. Is anything more beautiful than the face of a man or woman, boy or girl, who is made in the likeness of God?

Many years ago, I watched a documentary that was partly about how *National Geographic* assembles each issue of its iconic magazine. In those days, at least, the cover photograph was chosen by the editor in chief, who rapidly reviewed a display of the best pictures, quickly pointed at his favorites to narrow down the list, and then selected the final image—all in a matter of minutes. The editor said that what he chose most often was a human face because that is the most compelling image in the world. The Bible calls that image what it is: the likeness of God.

Inner Beauty

When we think about the beauty of humanity, however, we need to look beyond the merely physical to include the moral, relational, emotional, and spiritual dimensions of human personhood. Beauty really is more than skin deep! It is the totality of who we are. The image of God is not something we have, therefore, but

9 Dubay, *Evidential Power of Beauty*, 232.

who we are. The beauty of God's likeness in us can include everything from the sacrifices that parents make for their children to the unexpected reconciliation of long-estranged friends. Yet our physical appearance tends to be both the first thing that people notice about us and also one of the main things they evaluate. Thus, we focus on external beauty. Typically, our assessments of others are unflattering, and our verdicts about ourselves are harsh.

Knowing how obsessed people can get with outward appearances, the apostle Peter offered this wise caution:

> Do not let your adorning be external—the braiding of hair and the putting on of gold jewelry, or the clothing you wear—but let your adorning be the hidden person of the heart with the imperishable beauty of a gentle and quiet spirit, which in God's sight is very precious. (1 Pet. 3:3–4)

Peter was speaking specifically to women when he wrote this, but his application is for everyone. He was not saying that we should never get a stylish haircut or put a ring on one of our fingers or wear nice clothes. But he was saying that in comparison to nourishing the inward beauty of the human heart, we should never allow outward appearances to become our priority. "Inward beauty is more comely than exterior ornament," said Bernard of Clairvaux, "more even than the power of kings."[10]

Here is one simple way for us to test whether inner or outer beauty is more important to us. All we need to do is ask whether we spend more time and energy on physical fitness and personal

---

10 Bernard of Clairvaux, quoted in Farley, *Faith and Beauty*, 43.

grooming than we do on prayer and Bible study, which are the beauty enhancers of the Holy Spirit. Are we working harder on what is inside us or on what people see from the outside? Does who we *are* matter more to us or who people *think* we are? True beauty works its way from the inside out.

Beauty Broken

As soon as we start thinking seriously about what is inside us, we realize that we are not as beautiful as we were meant to be—not at all. Like David, we were born to be beautiful. Beauty is our destiny, which is one of the main purposes for this book: to help get us ready for eternity. Unfortunately, in this present moment—when we are caught between what we are and what we were made to be—we are all faced every day with the ugliness of humanity's fallen condition.

This is true physically. Even the world's most beautiful people cannot stay beautiful. We all face the long, slow, inevitable decline of our physical powers, which is one of the surest signs that we are living in a world that is under the judgment of God and destined one day to die.

The way we respond to beauty is ugly too. We turn physical appearance into an idol—whether our own beauty or the beauty of the person we want to have for ourselves—and this unleashes dark powers of destruction. "Man is seldom content to witness beauty," said Grand Chief Michael Somare, former Prime Minister of Papua New Guinea; "he must possess it."[11] Then, in our

---

11 Michael Somare, quoted in the front matter of Kirk Wallace Johnson, *The Feather Thief: Beauty, Obsession, and the Natural History Heist of the Century* (New York: Penguin, 2019).

efforts to steal something that God always meant to be a gift, we end up abusing it or destroying it. Just ask Bathsheba, Tamar, or Vashti—beautiful women from the Bible who were shamefully abused and cast aside.[12]

When we are not busy destroying beauty, we are guilty of disregarding it. We judge people on the basis of what we think is or is not beautiful. We overlook the variegated beauty of people from other ethnic backgrounds. Or we devalue people who are deformed. With disabled persons specifically in mind, Jean Vanier writes, "As soon as we start selecting and judging people instead of welcoming them as they are—with their sometimes hidden beauty, as well as their more frequent visible weaknesses—we are reducing life, not fostering it."[13] Our misperceptions of gender are a problem too. Women the world over "are perceived and judged, advantaged or disadvantaged, by their appearance in ways that men are not"—a problem that is greatly exacerbated by mainstream and social media.[14] Whoever we are, when people see us as unattractive and therefore unworthy of affection, it profoundly damages our sense of self-worth.

There is also the ugliness of death, which turns all our beautiful bodies into dust. Usually, we try to ignore this painful reality, but there is nothing beautiful about the end of life. In fact, the beauty of our humanity makes death all the more painful, for the loss of any beautiful life feels like an infinite grief. This pain is part of the backstory to the sculpture I mentioned at the

12 See 2 Sam. 11; 13:1–14; Est. 1.

13 Jean Vanier, quoted in Devan Joy Stahl and Maggi Jones, "Jean Vanier on Beauty and Disability," *Journal of Disability and Religion* 24, no. 2 (2020): 229–48.

14 Goldberg, "Who Gets to Judge?," 6.

beginning of this chapter. When my mother-in-law Elaine first saw Kirsten Kokkin's image of a beautiful boy in the hands of God, she turned and walked right out of the gallery. The artwork reminded her instantly of a loss that she grieved almost every day—the infant death of her firstborn son—and thus she could not bear to look at a perfect baby boy.

Wherever we turn, beauty seems to be broken. But the most tragic loss of beauty is within us. Plotinus—a wise philosopher of the third century AD—grimly yet accurately described the human soul as

> ugly, ill-disciplined and unjust, full of cravings and all kinds of disturbance, in the midst of fears because of cowardice, and of jealousies of petty-mindedness, thinking of everything in so far as it thinks of them at all, as mortal and lowly, twisted in every respect, in love with pleasures that are impure.[15]

If Plotinus's description sounds familiar, it is because our ugliness also turns out to be more than skin deep. Jesus used a horrific image to describe our inner lack of beauty—especially when we claim to follow God but our hearts are far away from him. He said, "Woe to you, scribes and Pharisees, hypocrites! For you are like whitewashed tombs, which outwardly appear beautiful, but within are full of dead people's bones and all uncleanness" (Matt. 23:27). Sometimes a fair visage is merely the death mask for a vicious soul.

To summarize, in so many ways beauty turns out to be one of our biggest problems, physically and spiritually, socially and

---

15 Plotinus, *Ennead 1.6: On Beauty*, trans. Andrew Smith (Las Vegas, NV: Parmenides, 2016), 53–54.

personally. We "live in a world that is achingly beautiful," concludes N. T. Wright, and at the same time "awesomely ugly."[16] Will we have to live with this paradox forever, or does God have a better destiny in mind for us?

Beautiful Again

Thank God, there is a way for us to become beautiful again—and for the whole creation to become beautiful with us. The process begins simply with confessing our sins and trusting Jesus for forgiveness through his blood, shed on the cross, which cleanses us from all our ugly sins. But it does not end there. Remember, beauty is your destiny! The God who has promised to make "a new heaven and a new earth" (Rev. 21:1) has also promised to make a new *you*! On the last of all days, when we finally see Jesus face-to-face, we will become beautiful as he is, body and soul.

Thankfully, we do not have to wait to start becoming more beautiful. The sanctification we experience already in this life commences God's beautification of our souls. In Ephesians 4, where the apostle Paul writes about putting off the old self and putting on the new self, he describes our renewal as a re-creation "after the likeness of God in true righteousness and holiness" (Eph. 4:22–24). In other words, in Christ we are created back into the image of God. And because the image of God is beautiful, our renewal after his divine likeness restores our inner beauty. Writing in the fourth century, Basil of Caesarea expressed this promise as an imperative: "Be cleansed of the filth with which sin has covered

---

16 N. T. Wright, quoted in Alison Krivickas and Kimberly Miller, "The Journey Within: Imagination and the Art of Spiritual Formation," *Seen Journal* 15, no. 2 (2015): 10.

you, and find again your natural beauty, as you would restore an image to its original condition by cleaning it."[17]

The connection between sanctification and beautification makes all the more sense when we remember that to sanctify is to make holy and that holiness is essential to divine beauty—what Jonathan Edwards called God's "peculiar beauty."[18] Holiness can become our peculiar beauty too. As we become more sanctified, we become more beautiful and come to share in God's "moral excellency, which is properly the beauty of the divine nature."[19] This beautification is the work specifically of the third person of the Trinity, God's beautiful Spirit, who is the agent of our sanctification. When Jesus breathed on his disciples and said, "Receive the Holy Spirit" (John 20:22), he was beginning our beautification.

This Spirit-empowered process confronts us with one of the great paradoxes of the Christian life. At the same time that our bodies, inevitably, are becoming less beautiful, God can do a work of grace that so beautifies our souls that our lives display more and more of his beauty. The Bible says that even though "our outer self is wasting away, our inner self is being renewed day by day" (2 Cor. 4:16). In other words, it is possible for us simultaneously to become more decrepit outwardly and yet inwardly more dazzling.

As a pastor, I have met many people who radiate divine beauty. Few of them were beautiful according to conventional

---

17 Basil of Caesarea, quoted in Martin Schleske, *The Sound of Life's Unspeakable Beauty*, trans. Janet Gesme (Grand Rapids, MI: Eerdmans, 2020), 317.

18 Jonathan Edwards, *A Treatise concerning Religious Affections*, quoted in Patrick Sherry, *Spirit and Beauty: An Introduction to Theological Aesthetics*, 2nd ed. (London: SCM, 2002), 33.

19 Jonathan Edwards, *Ethical Writings*, quoted in Sherry, *Spirit and Beauty*, 13.

standards for physical appearance, but all of them had a glowing countenance that seemed to shine with the light of their inner beauty. Some were younger souls whose lives were cut short by tragedy. But most of them were older saints—some with acute physical limitations, chronic pains, and debilitating medical conditions—whom the Holy Spirit had been making more beautiful for their entire lives. When I was with them, I sensed that they were bringing me closer to the presence of God, and I wanted to linger.

These beautiful saints inspire me to believe that there is still hope for me. I am not yet the person I want to be (although, thank God, I am not the person I used to be either). Thankfully, the Holy Spirit is not finished with my beautification, which means that with patience and perseverance, a more beautiful "me" will still emerge. By God's grace it will be the "me" that Peter wrote about: "the hidden person of the heart" who has "the imperishable beauty of a gentle and quiet spirit, which in God's sight is very precious" (1 Pet. 3:4).

Violin maker Martin Schleske has spent most of his career not only handcrafting exceptional stringed instruments but also reflecting on the spiritual lessons that he learns from them. Concerning our sanctification, he writes,

> What moves me is the idea that God has the heart of an artist, who does not force reality into submission by bending and breaking and going against the grain. The thought of seeing every person, ourselves included, as a unique work of art in progress, an ever-changing and matchless expression of God, changes everything.

Then Schleske asks a hope-filled question that has as many answers as there are beautiful, beloved children of God: "What is now in the making?"[20]

Saving Beauty

Everything the Bible says about our beauty, ugliness, and eventual beautification has manifold implications for the way we live today. Here I mention only two of many important areas for application: ethics and the arts.

Let me start with ethics. If it is true that we are beautifully and wonderfully made, then we must—simply *must*—respect our bodies as temples for the Holy Spirit. We are not gnostics, who deny the goodness of creation; on the contrary, we believe that bodies are good. Nor are we aesthetic elitists: we believe that *all* bodies are good, including our own. The inherent goodness of our bodies calls us to lifelong stewardship of our physical wellness as an important aspect of our service to God. John Calvin argued that "since God created our bodies as well as our souls, and nourishes and maintains them, this is good enough reason why he should be served and honored with our bodies."[21] Christian philosopher Roger Scruton provides a further rationale for the stewardship of our physical selves when he writes,

> My body is not my property but—to use the theological term— my incarnation. My body is not an object but a subject, just as

20 Schleske, *Life's Unspeakable Beauty*, 99–100.
21 Calvin, *Against the Nicodemites*, quoted in W. David O. Taylor, *The Theater of God's Glory: Calvin, Creation, and the Liturgical Arts* (Grand Rapids, MI: Eerdmans, 2017), 98.

I am. I don't own it, any more than I own myself. I am inextricably mingled with it, and what is done to my body is done to me.[22]

The sacredness of our physicality has implications for how we treat other people too. What a difference it makes when we look at each and every human being and say, "Now there is a beautiful person, fearfully and wonderfully made in the image of my beautiful God." Our calling to love one another is a call to see his beauty in one another and then to treat one another with the holy reverence that sacred beauty demands.

If we are beautifully and wonderfully made, then we must—simply *must*—respect each person's dignity. There are many reasons to oppose any form of sinful prejudice against other persons—on the basis of religion or worldview; on the basis of race, ethnicity, or nationality; on the basis of age, class, or station in society; on the basis of sex or gender or sexuality; on the basis of ability or disability. This is profoundly wrong for many reasons, but here is one of the most important: it is a failure to recognize the inherent beauty of every person made in the likeness of God. When, for whatever reason, we conclude that someone does not deserve our care or respect, this is a form of sacrilege against the holy artistry of God, who has set his image—however distorted it may become—in every human being. Disrespecting another human being is wrong because, according to one contemporary liturgy, "God's work in creation is too wonderful, too ancient, too beautiful, too good to be desecrated."[23]

22 Roger Scruton, *Beauty: A Very Short Introduction* (Oxford: Oxford University Press, 2011), 137.

23 Presbyterian Church (USA), "Call to Restore the Creation," General Assembly (1990), quoted in Belden C. Lane, *Ravished by Beauty: The Surprising Legacy of Reformed Spirituality* (Oxford: Oxford University Press, 2011), 19.

If we are beautifully and wonderfully made, then we must—simply *must*—also safeguard human life. There are many reasons to oppose abortion, but here is one of the most important: every unborn child is beautiful in the sight of God. The same is true of every victim of unlawful gun violence or survivor of sexual abuse. Every human being is an embodiment of divine beauty. This is a basic norm for human rights. Therefore, we rightly regard the physical harm of any innocent person as a sacrilege—a violation of sacred, divine beauty.

Reimagining Beauty

Beauty is also a basic norm for Christians in the arts. As people made in the image of God—and even more as people remade in the image of Jesus Christ—aesthetic awareness is an integral aspect of who we are. We are, after all, God's "workmanship" (Eph. 2:10), which is a good translation for the Greek word *poiēma*, from which we derive the English word *poem*. As masterpieces of God's artistry, we have been made and remade to become artists ourselves—not for art's sake but for God's sake.

Unlike God, of course, we cannot create something out of nothing. We can, however, make something out of what God has made, working within its potentialities to bring out its beauty. The philosopher Elaine Scarry simply yet profoundly expresses one of art's primary impulses when she asserts, "Beauty prompts a copy of itself." Scarry proceeds to claim that this is especially true in our response to beautiful people: "Beauty . . . prompts the begetting of children: when the eye sees someone beautiful, the whole body wants to reproduce the person."[24] One of the many ways we bear

24 Elaine Scarry, *On Beauty and Being Just* (Princeton, NJ: Princeton University Press, 1999), 4.

witness to the wonder of our creation, therefore, is in the way we represent the human form. Think, for example, of the celebrated paintings of Kehinde Wiley—the creator, most famously, of the official portraits of Barack and Michelle Obama—which draw on the grand traditions of the old masters but also reinterpret them to depict the beauty and dignity of African Americans in their everyday lives. Wiley's paintings demonstrate that we are fearfully and wonderfully made.

This does not mean that artists are called to make only beautiful things. The world is more complicated than that—and more broken. Yet the truest artists never lose sight of our divine beauty, even when they also feel compelled to reveal the ugly side of life. Art has the redemptive power to take into account humanity's suffering while at the same time showing us the hope of healing. The Dutch theologian Abraham Kuyper asserted that "art has the mystical task of reminding us in its productions of the beautiful that was lost and of anticipating its perfect coming luster."[25] Thinking along similar lines, art historian John Walford advocates for artists to display a "broken beauty" that "is not only true to the human condition but can embody the essence of the gospel of redemption." Such art, Walford says, portrays "a redemptive beauty, which acknowledges suffering while preserving hope."[26]

Hope is what Elaine Maxwell experienced when she finally found the courage to walk back into a Denver art gallery and take

25 Abraham Kuyper, "Calvinism and Art," in *Calvinism: Six Stone Foundation Lectures* (1898; repr., Grand Rapids, MI: Eerdmans, 1943), 155.

26 E. John Walford, "The Case for a Broken Beauty: An Art Historical Viewpoint," in *The Beauty of God: Theology and the Arts*, ed. Daniel J. Treier, Mark Husbands, and Roger Lundin (Downers Grove, IL: IVP Academic, 2007), 109.

another look at Kirsten Kokkin's sculpture of a baby in the hands of God. Recall that the death of her only son when he was still a newborn caused my mother-in-law at first to turn away from a work of art depicting a perfect baby boy. After taking some time to step outside and grieve, however, she was persuaded to go back inside for a second look. She did more than simply look. In spite of her suffering—and perhaps because of it—her heart was ready to bring the artwork home.

Through her tears, Elaine realized that the sculpture was more than a sad reminder of what she had lost. It was also an image of her son as a person made in the image of God and therefore an image of beauty. It was a witness that we are, each of us, God's handiwork, knit together by nimble divine fingers in our mother's womb. Kokkin's sculpture became for Elaine a healing assurance that God always keeps his beautiful people in his care, including the loved ones we have lost. It also became a resurrection vision of our glorious destiny, holding the lustrous promise of the eternal beauty we will behold and become when our lowly bodies rise again at the return of our Lord Jesus Christ.

Therefore a man shall leave his father and his mother and hold fast to his wife, and they shall become one flesh.

GENESIS 2:24

Because of the Spirit who indwells it, the human body belongs to the realm of Christ's resurrected body and therefore again should be consecrated in anticipation of its full participation in that realm.

W. DAVID O. TAYLOR

5

When Sex Is Beautiful

The Beauty of Purity

JONATHAN EDWARDS HAD A PASSION for beauty, as we have seen. He adored the beauty of the triune God that he saw revealed everywhere in the world around him. As a young man and a new convert, Edwards often went out alone into the woods near his home in Hartford County, Connecticut, marveling at the beauty he witnessed and singing God's praises as he walked along.

Imagine how fascinated Edwards must have been to learn about a girl who sounded like a kindred spirit. She lived fifty miles away—about two days' journey on horseback. In one of his journals, Edwards wrote down what he had heard about her:

> They say there is a young lady in [New Haven] who is beloved of that Great Being, who made and rules the world, and that there are certain seasons in which the Great Being . . . comes to her and fills her mind with exceeding sweet delight, and

that she hardly cares for anything except to meditate on him. . . . She will sometimes go about from place to place, singing sweetly and seems to be always full of joy and pleasure; and no one knows for what. She loves to be alone, walking in the fields and groves, and seems to have someone invisible always conversing with her.[1]

Needless to say, Edwards made his way to New Haven to meet this remarkable young woman: Miss Sarah Pierpont. In their shared love for divine beauty, Jonathan and Sarah fell in love, were married, and as partners in ministry raised eleven children. First captivated by creation to see the beauty of God, they also saw the beauty in one another and wanted to share their lives—soul, spirit, and body.

Embodied Humanity

Yes, *body*. The Christian faith is not merely spiritual but comes to full expression when we honor God with our bodies. Nowhere is this more evident and potentially more beautiful than in our sexuality. The marriage of Sarah and Jonathan Edwards is one example of the physical-sexual-spiritual union that goes all the way back to the garden of Eden, when God said, "Therefore a man shall leave his father and his mother and hold fast to his wife, and they shall become one flesh" (Gen. 2:24). When a man and a woman make sacred promises to one another—the vows that form the bonds of covenant matrimony—and then give themselves to one another, they are joined together both spiritually and sexually.

---

1   Jonathan Edwards, quoted in Belden C. Lane, *Ravished by Beauty: The Surprising Legacy of Reformed Spirituality* (Oxford: Oxford University Press, 2011), 173.

The Bible tells us that this is beautiful—so beautiful that we cannot do justice either to beauty or to humanity's creation in God's image without talking about sexuality. We first see this beauty in the garden of Eden, when Adam takes one look at Eve and says,

This at last is bone of my bones
    and flesh of my flesh. (Gen. 2:23)

Adam saw his complement—what John Milton called "his other self"—and immediately he wanted to unite with her.

We see the beauty of sex in some of the love stories that the Bible tells, such as Jacob's enduring devotion to Rachel (Gen. 29:18) or Boaz's chaste and generous embrace of Ruth after their memorable night together during the barley harvest (Ruth 3). We see the beauty of sexuality when wise Agur marvels at the world's great mysteries—things he cannot understand because they are "too amazing"—and concludes his list with "the way of a man with a young woman" (Prov. 30:18–19 NIV). But maybe we see it most clearly of all in the Song of Songs. This beautiful book gives us the lyrics for an album of love songs about a couple who went through all the ups (and most of the downs) of a passionate romance before joyfully consummating their desires behind the holy door of their marriage chamber.

These are only glimpses. The Bible does not give us a guide to sex or explain all the reasons why it is a beautiful part of God's creation. It simply shows us the one and only God-given context for sexual intimacy—that is, within a biblically defined marriage—together with clear commands for avoiding any form of sexual misconduct that will misuse our bodies and harm our souls. Apart from these basics, we are left to infer why and how sex is beautiful, or at least why and how it *can* be beautiful.

It is easy to get the mistaken impression that when it comes to our sexuality, God is mainly concerned about making sure that we follow his list of dos and don'ts—especially the don'ts. In fact, God is more concerned about the beauty of the why and the joy he knows will come to us when we offer our physical bodies (including our sexual selves) for his glory.

Glory is the theme of the apostle Paul's remarkable teaching about sex and the body in 1 Corinthians 6. Apparently, the sex-crazed Corinthians had been misled into thinking that because our spiritual lives belong to another world, what we do with our bodies does not matter. Even having sex with a prostitute is permissible, they thought. Paul condemns their casual promiscuity by saying, "The body is not meant for sexual immorality, but for the Lord" (1 Cor. 6:13). He also insists that our bodies—not simply our souls—are temples for the Holy Spirit (1 Cor. 6:19). What we do with our bodies, therefore, has a deep spiritual purpose as one part of what we give to God. Paul thus concludes with this clear exhortation: "Glorify God in your body" (1 Cor. 6:20).

Sex in Marriage

Sex is beautiful whenever we honor God with our bodies. This happens most obviously when a husband and wife share sexual intimacy. I use the verb "share" deliberately. People more commonly talk about "having" sex, which seems to put the emphasis on what we can get for ourselves. Would it not make more sense to talk about "sharing" or "giving" sex? Marital intercourse is beautiful when it is self-giving instead of self-loving—when God-honoring pleasure is generously offered rather than exclusively received or selfishly demanded.

Theologians have long distinguished between different kinds of love. C. S. Lewis famously wrote about this in his book *The Four Loves*, in which he described *storgē*, *philia*, *agapē*, and *erōs* as the Greek words for affection, friendship, charity, and romantic love, respectively. *Erōs*, of course, is romantic, sexual desire. *Agapē* is the innovative vocabulary word that the New Testament uses to designate selfless, sacrificial love. These various terms for love help us see how beautiful it is when sexual desire is united with selfless love: *erōs* plus *agapē*. There is nothing casual about beautiful sex in the context of marriage, where it is divinely intended to become an embodied expression of covenant love.

The Puritan Thomas Hooker captured the flavor of this more complete love in his description of a godly man whose heart has been captivated by his betrothed:

> The man whose heart is endeared to the woman he loves, he dreams of her in the night, hath her in his eye & apprehension when he awakes, museth on her as he sits at table, walks with her when he travels and parlies with her in each place where he [converses]; . . . the heart of the lover keeps company with the beloved.[2]

What Hooker said about a man in love is equally true for a woman in love, of course. When couples share their lives, not

---

2   Thomas Hooker, *The Application of Redemption*, quoted in Lane, *Ravished by Beauty*, 107.

just their bedrooms, sex becomes beautiful. In her personal narrative *Sex and the City of God*, Carolyn Weber specifies what is at stake in sharing sexual intimacy: "When we enter another body, we enter another life. We enter another's joys and sorrows, needs and wants."[3] Only the marriage promises of self-giving love can bear the weight of such a total life commitment.

What else can we say about the possible beauty of married sexuality? It is beautiful because the human body is beautiful, made in the image of God. It is beautiful when it is fruitful, as God originally intended (see Gen. 1:28), producing the gift of children, who are also made in the image of God.

Married sex is most beautiful when it tells the gospel story. Here we encounter an extraordinary mystery that is essential to understanding not only God's design for our sexuality but also his entire plan of redemption. The relationship between husband and wife—including their one-flesh union—is intended to illustrate our saving love relationship with Jesus Christ. We know this because when the apostle Paul quotes Genesis 2:24 to the Ephesians ("Therefore a man shall leave his father and mother and hold fast to his wife, and the two shall become one flesh," Eph. 5:31), he adds a surprising editorial comment: "This mystery is profound, and I am saying that it refers to Christ and the church" (Eph. 5:32). If we have any doubt about the validity of this connection, all we need to do is turn to the last few pages of the Bible and see how our story ends (Rev. 19:6–9; 21:1–2). There we read about a match made in heaven: Jesus is the groom, and the church is his bride—happily ever after.

---

3   Carolyn Weber, *Sex and the City of God: A Memoir of Love and Longing* (Downers Grove, IL: InterVarsity Press, 2020), 176.

Sex is beautiful when it communicates this gospel narrative. Paul calls married sexual intimacy a mystery because it lifts us beyond what is merely physical to signal something transcendent. Here it helps to remember that because our bodies are made in the image of God, they always carry spiritual meaning. This is especially true of a believer's body, which is united to the risen Christ and therefore destined to become immortal. When husband and wife selflessly love one another with bodies that are consecrated for the coming resurrection, together they are living into the gospel story.

In his book *Our Bodies Tell God's Story*, Christopher West summarizes the significance of sexual intimacy:

> The body is not only biological; since we were made in the image of God, male and female, the body is also theological. It tells an astounding divine story. And it does so precisely through the mystery of sexual differences and the call of the two to become "one flesh." This means that when we get the body and sex wrong, we get the divine story wrong too.[4]

West is wise to give us this warning. When it comes to our sexuality, there are many things that it is easy for us to get wrong. Happily, the reverse is also true. When we get the body right and sex right, we have an opportunity to get the gospel right too. Our lives bear witness to the passionate love of our Savior Jesus Christ and fulfill our communal calling to become his pure, eternal bride. Sex then communicates a message of salvation, in which our hearts are married to Christ's heart.

---

4 Christopher West, *Our Bodies Tell God's Story: Discovering the Divine Plan for Love, Sex, and Gender* (Grand Rapids, MI: Brazos, 2020), 5.

When Sex Is Not Beautiful

Several times so far in this chapter, I have come close to saying simply, "Sex is beautiful." Instead, I have added a qualifier, such as sex *can* be beautiful or it is *possible* for sex to be beautiful or sex is beautiful *when* . . . This is because—like everything else in this fallen world—our sexuality is damaged and distorted. Often, the most beautiful gifts become the most painful when they are scarred by sin, and this is surely true of our sexuality.

In speaking about sex, therefore, we need to ask once again a question that has troubled us repeatedly in our biblical, theological, and practical consideration of beauty. If our sexuality is divinely designed to express eternal beauty, then why does our actual experience with sex fall so far short of that ideal? Why do we go off script from the gospel story, in which sex is for the glory of God, and decide to tell our own story instead?

The simple answer is that too often we want the pleasures of sin more than we want the beauty of God. There are many ways to talk about sexual perversion and the damage it does. Sexual sin—in whatever form—is a rejection of clear biblical truth and a transgression of God's holy law. It may also be a violation of the natural order. All this is true. But sexual sin is also *ugly*, which ought to be reason enough to choose a different path.

Sex is ugly whenever it betrays a trust or breaks a promise. So is any and every form of sexual abuse: rape, sex trafficking, prostitution, incest, domestic violence, and so on. The physical harm and personal exploitation of another human being—usually, though not always, a woman—can never be anything except a grotesque violation of the beautiful image of God.

This is all the more true when sexual abuse is sanctioned by or secretly harbored in the church, with devastating results in the lives of the survivors and everyone else whose trust is betrayed as a result. Sex is ugly whenever it is treated as a physical act that can somehow be separated from the rest of life. Nancy Pearcey wisely criticizes the regnant view of sex as "an exchange of physical services between autonomous disconnected individuals." Although Christians typically "think sexual hedonism places too much value on the purely physical dimension" of life, she says, "in reality it places a very low value on the body, draining it of moral and personal significance."[5]

Pornography is ugly for some of the same reasons—and many more. Because it portrays human bodies, with their inherent beauty, sexual imagery may sometimes tempt us into thinking that we are looking at something beautiful. But we are deceived. As an industry of exploitation—virtually a slave trade[6]—pornography teaches viewers to see other people merely as objects of selfish desire rather than as real persons with eternal souls. This sad reality led the late philosopher Roger Scruton boldly and accurately to declare that pornography "is not a tribute to human beauty but a desecration of it."[7] Scruton said this because he believed that sexual desire is "an incandescent revelation of what you are." To "treat it as a commodity," therefore, "is to damage both present

---

5 Nancy Pearcey, *Love Thy Body: Answering Hard Questions about Life and Sexuality* (Grand Rapids, MI: Baker, 2018), 28.

6 Ray Ortlund, *The Death of Porn: Men of Integrity Building a World of Nobility* (Wheaton, IL: Crossway, 2021), 17–18. Ortlund argues further that because pornography involves human servitude, working to eradicate it is a justice issue.

7 Roger Scruton, *Beauty: A Very Short Introduction* (Oxford: Oxford University Press, 2011), 138.

self and future other."[8] In other words, pornography harms the viewer immediately, but eventually it hurts other people too. The way it teaches us to treat people—not the people on the screen but the real people we live with every day—is selfish and therefore far from beautiful.

What about masturbation? Much could be said about this subject too, about self-stimulation as self-worship that wastes away our spiritual and sexual powers. For now, the only question I want to ask is whether masturbation is beautiful. The answer is no because it is focused on having and taking, not giving and sharing.

Notice what various forms of sexual transgression have in common: they fail to express enduring love. Rather than cherishing another person, they use or abuse another person. Only loving actions are truly beautiful—the things we do for others and not simply for ourselves. Any time we take sex, keep sex, use sex, or steal sex, we are not giving or sharing it in the beautiful way that God intends.

Understanding this dynamic gives us something new to say to ourselves and maybe to others whenever we are tempted to sin in sexual ways. We can always say, "This is wrong," of course, or, "I shouldn't do this." But we can also say, "This isn't beautiful the way Jesus wants it to be, and I want my life—I want your life, I want our lives—to be more beautiful."

Knowing when sex is not beautiful also gives us another way to pray when we stumble and fall into sin, as we all do. First, we repent, not waiting even one more minute to ask God to forgive

---

8   Scruton, *Beauty*, 137.

our sins for Jesus's sake. By the power of the cross and the empty tomb, no sexual sin—no transgression of any kind—is too great for his grace. Then we ask God to help us "go, and sin no more" (John 8:11 KJV). "Make me holy, Lord"—that is something we can always pray. But we can also pray this: "Lord, by your gracious Spirit, make me strong to stand against Satan. And make my life more beautiful—sexually beautiful for you." The Holy Spirit will not wait another minute either but will start making us stronger, holier, and therefore more beautiful right away.

Sexual Sacrifice

At this point I need to expand on what I mean when I say that sex is beautiful. I am not referring primarily or exclusively to physical acts of sexual intimacy—more specifically, to sexual relations between a husband and a wife who are bound together by covenant promises. Such sex is (or can be) beautiful. That is not, however, the only way our sexuality can be beautiful for God. There is another form of sexual beauty that is more common—something that can be expressed by anyone, regardless of marital status, sex, age, or sexual orientation. I refer to the beauty of chastity: the sacrificial beauty of refraining from sex outside the bonds of covenant promise.

Admittedly, such purity seems contrary to our natural inclinations. At the end of her bestselling book *Sex in History,* Reay Tannahill writes, "The truth is that there has never been a very close match between human instincts and Judeo-Christian sexual morality."[9] Tannahill is right: what *we* want for us and what *God*

---

9   Reay Tannahill, *Sex in History,* quoted in Weber, *Sex and the City of God,* 206.

wants for us often feel contradictory. Christ's call to chastity is especially countercultural in today's oversexed culture, where cohabitation—so unwisely!—has become the norm, even among many churchgoers.[10] A call for celibacy in the life of a single Christian can come across like a consolation prize. Pursuing sexual purity is a hard struggle. Many of us can relate to Mother Teresa's reply when she was asked if it was hard to keep her vow of chastity. "Yes," she said, "I find it sometimes very difficult to smile at my spouse, Jesus, because He can be very demanding—sometimes."[11]

Yet the demand for sexual purity is the unmistakable teaching of Scripture, and therefore it must be God's permanent will for our lives. Notice how plainly and directly Paul says this to the Thessalonians:

> This is the will of God, your sanctification: that you abstain from sexual immorality, that each one of you know how to control his own body in holiness and honor, not in the passion of lust like the Gentiles who do not know God; that no one transgress and wrong his brother [or sister] in this matter, because the Lord is an avenger in all these things, as we told you beforehand and solemnly warned you. For God has not called us for impurity, but in holiness. Therefore whoever disregards this, disregards not man but God, who gives his Holy Spirit to you. (1 Thess. 4:3–8)

10　According to David J. Ayers, more than half of self-identified evangelical Protestants in America live together before they get married. Ayers, "The Cohabitation Dilemma Comes for America's Pastors," *Christianity Today*, April 2021, 37–41. See also Joe Carter, "Survey: Half of U.S. 'Christians' Say Casual Sex Is Acceptable," The Gospel Coalition, May 1, 2021, https://www.thegospelcoalition.org/.

11　Mother Teresa of Calcutta, quoted in Weber, *Sex and the City of God*, 50.

That last phrase is crucial—the part where Paul promises us the Holy Spirit. It is also life changing. The gift of God's beautiful Holy Spirit means that we have the power to resist temptation—including sexual temptation—and to live in a way that is holy for God. John Calvin highlighted our responsibility to cooperate with the Spirit's sanctification of our sexuality when he wrote,

> Ever since the Holy Spirit dedicated us as temples to God, we must take care that God's glory shine through us, and must not commit anything to defile ourselves with the filthiness of sin. Ever since both our souls and bodies are destined for heavenly incorruption and an unfading crown, we ought to strive manfully to keep them pure and uncorrupted until the Day of the Lord.[12]

We unleash extraordinary spiritual power and witness stunning beauty when as believers we make an uncompromising commitment to sexual purity and offer our bodies as living sacrifices for the glory of God (see Rom. 12:1–2). Remember that we did not make ourselves. God made us in his holy and divine image. Remember too that we were "bought with a price" (1 Cor. 6:20), which Jesus paid in blood to wash away our sins. Our bodies do not belong to us, therefore; we are not our own. Even though our culture tells us that we have a right to do whatever we want, with whomever we want, whenever we want to do it, the truth is that our bodies belong to God, both by creation and by redemption.

12 John Calvin, *Institutes of the Christian Religion*, 3.6.3, quoted in W. David O. Taylor, *The Theater of God's Glory: Calvin, Creation, and the Liturgical Arts* (Grand Rapids, MI: Eerdmans, 2017), 137.

Our bodies are not our personal property; they are our stewardship responsibility.

If giving our bodies to God seems like a sacrifice, that is because it is. It is a sexual sacrifice! It is also a gift—a gift to God and to everyone else who is honored and protected by the holy choices we make with our bodies. This includes our spouse (or future spouse), if God provides us one. And like most willing sacrifices, this freely offered gift is beautiful—beautiful to God and beautiful to the world, if only we have the eyes to behold it.

One of the most remarkable testimonies of the costly beauty of sexual sacrifice comes from the life of Helen Roseveare, the pioneering English medical missionary to Congo whose sufferings bore global witness to the evangelical church. When Roseveare first came to Christ as a student at Cambridge University, she pledged herself to missionary work and explicitly presented her life for kingdom service. She went out into the countryside and offered this astonishing prayer: "O.K. God, today I mean it. Go ahead and make me more like Jesus, whatever the cost."[13]

In a time of civil war, Congolese terrorists overran her hospital and violated her. Roseveare would later testify that in those horrific moments she found consolation in recognizing that she was suffering with Christ and for Christ. Then, after suffering such ungodly abuse, she faced an unexpected temptation. Some survivors of abuse are repelled by sex, owing

13 Helen Roseveare, quoted in Justin Taylor, "A Woman of Whom the World Was Not Worthy: Helen Roseveare (1925–2016)," The Gospel Coalition, December 7, 2016, https://www.thegospelcoalition.org/.

to the trauma they have endured. Yet, with stunning transparency, Roseveare wanted fellow Christians to know that in the immediate aftermath of her attack, she experienced sexual desire more strongly. Remembering her fervent prayers to be more like Jesus, she once again had to surrender her sexuality—body and soul—back to Jesus in order to keep living the beautiful life she knew that God was calling her to live as a single missionary.

Sex is not just beautiful when it is shared in a marriage but any time it is totally surrendered to Jesus Christ, including when we refrain from sexual activity for the greater glory of God. As Ray Ortlund rightly observes, "Inactive sexuality is not nonsexuality. It is purposeful sexuality."[14] By the grace of God, what Helen Roseveare did is something that anyone can do at any moment in life: we can offer our sexuality to God. This means that both marriage *and* singleness are equally high callings. They are different, complementary ways to live out the beauty of a faithful, sacrificial life for the glory of God.

Theologian Beth Felker Jones helpfully connects the sexual sacrifices that all of us can make to declaring the good news of Jesus Christ:

> When we—by the grace and power of God—are able to practice faithfulness in marriage and celibacy in singleness, we use our bodies to tell the story of God's radical faithfulness. . . .
>
> Ultimately, sexuality is about doing one of the most exciting things we get to do as Christians. It is about obeying the

---

14 Ortlund, *Death of Porn*, 80.

command to "glorify God in your body" (1 Cor 6:20 NRSV) and testifying to the truth and power of the gospel story.[15]

Is It Worth It?

All this may seem very costly. It always does feel costly at the time to give up something we desire, such as sexual pleasure. So it is worth asking whether it is worth it. Is it worth it to turn away for a season from the temptations of sin? Is it worth it to choose a more beautiful life and wait for the promised day when we will become "a crown of beauty in the hand of the LORD" (Isa. 62:3)?

The best answer to that question was given in the upper room where Jesus shared one last supper with his disciples before he was tried and tortured and crucified on the cross of Calvary. Remember what Jesus said that night. He took a piece of bread, held it out to his first disciples—and to us—and said, "This is *my* body, which is given for you" (Luke 22:19).

Whenever we hear these words, we remember the beautiful sacrifice of love that saved the world. The cost of that sacrifice demanded that Jesus live a perfectly sinless life. He too was tempted by sexual sin—tempted as a single man. We do not know when, or how, or with whom, but we know that he too was tempted "in every way, just as we are" (Heb. 4:15 NIV), which surely includes sexual temptation. Jesus resisted this temptation and every temptation. This means that before he died a sacrificial death, Jesus lived a sacrificial life—in other words, a beautiful life.

15 Beth Felker Jones, "Sex," in *Life Questions Every Student Asks: Faithful Responses to Common Issues*, ed. Gary M. Burge and David Lauber (Downers Grove, IL: IVP Academic, 2020), 51, 61.

Now Jesus invites us to live a beautiful life—a chaste life—from this moment forward and every time we fall. He does more than invite; by his Spirit, he also empowers. It was specifically to sexual sinners, who were misusing their bodies, that the apostle Paul wrote, "You were washed, you were sanctified, you were justified in the name of the Lord Jesus Christ and by the Spirit of our God" (1 Cor. 6:11). When we live into the cleansing, sanctifying, justifying grace that God has for us in Jesus Christ, our lives—including our bodies—help tell the beautiful story of the gospel.

*And the Word became flesh and dwelt among us,
and we have seen his glory, glory as of the only
Son from the Father, full of grace and truth.*

JOHN 1:14

*There is scarcely anything that is excellent, beautiful,
pleasant, or profitable but what is used in the
Scripture as an emblem of Christ. . . . He is called
a rose and lily, and other such similitudes, because
of his transcendent beauty and fragrancy.*

JONATHAN EDWARDS

6

Beautiful Savior

The Beauty of God Incarnate

IT TOOK A LONG, LONG TIME for Augustine of Hippo to surrender his mind, heart, and will to Jesus Christ. But after wasting his younger years in idleness and dissolute living, he forsook his sinful ways and dedicated the remainder of his life to following Jesus.

Augustine took this step partly because he saw in the Son of God such a true and eternal beauty that he was compelled to bow down in worship. The beauty of Jesus changed his life, as it changes the life of anyone who trusts in him. Here is how Augustine described his newfound Savior, who is beautiful everywhere:

Beautiful as God, as the Word who is with God, he is beautiful in the Virgin's womb where he did not lose his godhead but assumed our humanity. Beautiful he is as a baby, as the Word unable to speak, because while he was still without speech, still a baby in arms and nourished at his mother's breast, the heavens spoke for him, a star guided the magi, and he was adored in the manger as food for the humble. He was beautiful in heaven, then, and beautiful on earth: beautiful in the womb, and beautiful in his parents' arms. He was beautiful in his miracles, but just as beautiful under the scourges, beautiful in laying down his life and beautiful in taking it up again, beautiful on the cross, beautiful in the tomb, and beautiful in heaven.[1]

Born Beautiful

According to Augustine, we catch our first glimpse of the beauty of Jesus in the stories of his birth. This means that Christmas truly is the most beautiful time of the year. The colors are beautiful—forest green, scarlet red, royal gold. The lights are beautiful, shining in the night. Many of the decorations are beautiful as well, especially the manger scenes. The music is also memorably beautiful. As we attend various concerts and late-night worship services, our hearts are touched by the lyrics of the old familiar carols. Brilliant new music is being written all the time in honor of the most celebrated birth in the history of the world. The vast quantity and stunning beauty of the world's Christmas music is a powerful apologetic in and of itself for the saving truth it celebrates.

Yet the true beauty of Christmas is not simply what we see and hear (and smell and taste) but the Son of God incarnate. As John the Evangelist reflected on his personal experience with Jesus

---

1   Augustine, on Ps. 44, in *Expositions of the Psalms*, vol. 2, *Psalms 33–50*, trans. Maria Boulding, ed. John E. Rotelle, part 3, vol. 16 of *Works of Saint Augustine: A Translation for the 21st Century* (Hyde Park, NY: New City Press, 2000), 283.

Christ, he wrote these words with a sense of wonder: "The Word became flesh and dwelt among us, and we have seen his glory, glory as of the only Son from the Father, full of grace and truth" (John 1:14). Because "glory" here refers to the visible radiance of the one and only Son of God, we might as well translate one of John's key phrases like this: "We have seen his beauty." Christmas is beautiful for the simple reason that Jesus is beautiful.

So far, we have seen that God is beautiful, creation is beautiful, and people created in God's image are beautiful, both male and female, including our sexuality. Now we behold an even greater beauty, as these wonders converge in the person of Jesus Christ. The culmination of all beauty—literally, its *apotheosis*—is the incarnate Son of God. He *is* the beauty of God in visible form, "the radiance of the glory of God" (Heb. 1:3). He *is* the fairest revelation in the created universe. He *is* humanity's perfect "image of the invisible God" (Col. 1:15), "the exact imprint of his nature" (Heb. 1:3). Down through the ages, the church has celebrated Christ's unique beauty. The early church father Clement of Alexandria declared, "Our Savior is beautiful to be loved by those who desire true beauty."[2] Similarly, the Eastern Orthodox saint Nicodemus lifted his eyes to heaven and exclaimed, concerning Christ, "O my God, if Thy creations are so full of beauty, delight and joy, how infinitely more full of beauty, delight and joy are Thou Thyself, Creator of all!"[3]

---

2   Clement of Alexandria, quoted in Patrick Sherry, *Spirit and Beauty: An Introduction to Theological Aesthetics*, 2nd ed. (London: SCM, 2002), 6.

3   Nicodemus of the Holy Mountain, quoted in Ann Voskamp, *One Thousand Gifts: A Dare to Live Fully Right Where You Are* (Grand Rapids, MI: Zondervan, 2010), 102.

Not So Beautiful

If the fairest of all beauties is the glory of the Son of God, how can we be more precise about the nature of his beauty, so that we see it for what it truly is and also for what it is not?

The beauty of the incarnation does not lie in the remarkable circumstances of our Savior's birth. Christmas, of all holidays, tends to get romanticized. This is true in all the Hallmark television specials, with their homey scenes and predictable plotlines. But the church also tends to romanticize the first Christmas. Admittedly, the star that led the magi to Mary's child must have been a rare object of celestial beauty—so too the heavenly angels and their glorious choruses. Even stable walls and manger hay sound charming in a Christmas carol, if stated poetically and set to the right melody. Yet there was nothing beautiful about a poor family making a long journey to Bethlehem at the whim of an imperial bureaucracy or about a problem pregnancy coming to term in an overcrowded barn or about a troop of rustic shepherds paying their respects in the middle of the night. Jesus was not born in beautiful surroundings, and he never lived in the lap of any luxury.

Nor was Jesus exceptionally beautiful in his physical appearance. Artists who render his birth in oil or charcoal or three-dimensional media strive valiantly to do him justice. Typically, they want Jesus to look beautiful. Yet the writers of the Gospels steadfastly refuse to describe the physical appearance of the newborn Christ or, for that matter, to help us imagine what he looked like at any age. This is remarkable. When we try to describe people to friends they have never met, we often start with their physical characteristics. But the Bible never provides any of that information for Jesus: his height, weight, skin tone, hair color, or facial features. We really have no idea what Jesus looked like. Thus, whatever is beautiful about him cannot be based on anything unusually attractive about his physical appearance.

In fact, the one place where the Bible *does* comment on his features seems to indicate that he was *un*attractive. In his song of the suffering servant, the prophet Isaiah says that the promised Savior "had no form or majesty that we should look at him, / and no beauty that we should desire him" (Isa. 53:2). John Oswalt's explanation of this verse is worth quoting at length:

> The Christian thinks inevitably of Jesus Christ: a baby born in the back-stable of a village inn. This would shake the Roman Empire? A man quietly coming to the great preacher of the day and asking to be baptized. This is the advent of the man who would be heralded as the Savior of the world? No, this is not what we think the arm of the Lord should look like. We were expecting a costumed drum major to lead our triumphal parade. Our eyes are caught and satisfied by superficial splendor. This man, says Isaiah, will have none of that. As a result, our eyes flicker across him in a crowd and we do not even see him. His splendor is not on the surface, and those who have no inclination to look beyond the surface will never even see him, much less pay him any attention.[4]

Rather than being sought out for his physical beauty by any earthly expectation, Jesus was rejected, and "as one from whom

---

4   John N. Oswalt, *The Book of Isaiah, Chapters 1–39*, New International Commentary on the Old Testament (Grand Rapids, MI: Eerdmans, 1986), 382–83.

men hide their faces / he was despised, and we esteemed him not" (Isa. 53:3). Possibly Isaiah was prophesying the disfigurement that Jesus suffered in his torture and execution. Yet the fact remains that the Bible studiously avoids calling attention to our Savior's physical beauty.

Of course, in his incarnation, Jesus had the same splendor that we all have. As we have seen, all of us bear the beauty of being fearfully and wonderfully made in the image and likeness of God. Doubtless when his mother Mary looked at Jesus through the eyes of love, she declared that the child in her arms was a "beautiful baby." There is *always* something beautiful in our embodied humanity, and this is strongly affirmed by the fact that God the Son took on our flesh, remaining fully divine and yet becoming fully a human being in sinew and bone. "Good is the flesh that the Word has become," writes Brian Wren in the title line of a recent Christmas carol, and "good is the pleasure of God in our flesh."[5] If we wish to specify what is distinctively beautiful about the incarnate Son of God, however, we must set aside the usual optics.

The Beauty of Humility

What *does* make Jesus so beautiful? Why did the prophet Isaiah say of the coming Savior that in his day "the LORD of hosts will be a crown of glory, / and a diadem of beauty, to the remnant of his people" (Isa. 28:5)? Why did John testify in the opening verses of his Gospel that he had seen the utterly unique glory-beauty of the one and only? Why do we say that Jesus Christ is beauty incarnate?

---

5   Brian Wren, "Good Is the Flesh" (Carol Stream, IL: Hope, 1989).

Consider, first of all, the beauty of our Lord's *humility*.[6] The simple fact of his humanity displays extraordinary condescension. In his very nature, Jesus was and is God. As the second person of the Trinity, he is God the Son eternal. Therefore, from eternity past he had lived in the absolute exaltation of his deity, adored by myriad angels and untouched by any pain or earthly sorrow. All the honor, all the glory, and all the praise belonged to him.

And yet, even "though he was in the form of God," the Scripture says, he "did not count equality with God a thing to be grasped, but emptied himself, by taking the form of a servant, being born in the likeness of men" (Phil. 2:6–7). Simply by becoming a human being, the everlasting Son of God performed the most astonishing act of personal humility that the world had ever witnessed. He did not divest himself of his deity when he became a man, but he did ungrasp its glories, and in doing so, he displayed new dimensions of humble beauty. As beautiful as he had always been in his divinity, by emptying himself Jesus revealed himself—paradoxically—to be even more beautiful.

Sam Storms has expressed Christ's beautiful humility in a series of paradoxes:

The Word became flesh!
God became human!
the invisible became visible!
the untouchable became touchable!
the transcendent one descended!

6   For a much fuller treatment of this subject, see Jonathan King, *The Beauty of the Lord: Theology as Aesthetics*, Studies in Historical and Systematic Theology (Bellingham, WA: Lexham, 2018), 152–72.

the unlimited became limited!
the infinite became finite!
the immutable became mutable!
the unbreakable became fragile!
eternity entered time!
the independent became dependent!
the almighty became weak!
the exalted was humbled!
fame turned into obscurity!
from power to weakness![7]

The way John expresses this paradox in his Gospel is striking. The evangelist declares that when the Word became flesh, he "dwelt among us." The verb that John chooses here is a form of the word *tabernacle*. To say this the way that we might say it in contemporary English, Jesus "pitched his tent" with us.

This expression explicitly calls to mind the tabernacle from the Old Testament—the portable sanctuary that the children of Israel made according to the precise instructions that God gave to Moses on Mount Sinai. The Israelites carried their grand tent with them through the wilderness for forty years before erecting it in the promised land (see Ex. 25–31; 35–40; Josh. 10:43; 18:1). This sacred tent of worship, or tabernacle, was the earthly dwelling place for the living God, symbolizing his presence with his people.

When Jesus was born, God took up residence (or "tabernacled") with his people in a new way. In his incarnation, God the Son

---

7 Sam Storms, "The Most Amazing Verse in the Bible," quoted in Andreas J. Kösten-berger and Alexander E. Stewart, *The First Days of Jesus: The Story of the Incarnation* (Wheaton, IL: Crossway, 2015), 13–14.

began—for the first time and forever—to dwell with us bodily. He did not just take on a body, points out Sam Allberry; he *became* a body, which surely is "the highest compliment the human body has ever been paid. God not only thought our bodies up and enjoyed putting several billion of them together; he made one for himself."[8] Furthermore, the incarnation was not reversible but permanent, which means that right now there is "a human body sitting at the right hand of God the Father at the very center of heaven."[9]

The embodiment of the Son of God meant that he would suffer physical pain, weariness, hunger and thirst, and indeed that he had become mortal. It also meant, however, that he would be able to come near to us in our struggles and empathize with our sorrows. In a testimony he wrote for the general public, Howard Kelly—who taught medicine at Johns Hopkins University in the early part of the twentieth century—bore witness to the "tenderness and nearness of God in Christ which satisfies the heart's longings, and shows me that the infinite God, Creator of the world, took our very nature upon Him that He might in infinite love be one with His people to redeem them."[10] This was all part of what it meant for Jesus to be born in our likeness, to become incarnate. He *gets* us!

When we understand what the Son of God gave up in order to enter into our humanity and when we consider the countless

8 Sam Allberry, *What God Has to Say about Our Bodies: How the Gospel Is Good News for Our Physical Selves* (Wheaton, IL: Crossway, 2021), 20.

9 Allberry, *Our Bodies*, 21.

10 Howard Kelly, quoted in Chris Gehrz, "My Favorite 'Fundamentalist,'" *Anxious Bench* (blog), *Patheos*, December 9, 2021, https://www.patheos.com/blogs/anxiousbench/.

indignities he endured in this fallen world, we bear witness to such astonishing humility that we feel compelled to say, "Jesus is beautiful!" Once we "come into contact with the manger at Bethlehem," marvels Thomas Dubay, we "cannot entirely escape the ineffable loveliness of the idea of the omnipotent God dwelling in the form of a feeble baby."[11]

The vast distance between heaven and earth enables us to see—much more clearly—what we ought to see when we look at the nativity. If we sentimentalize the birth of our Savior by transforming it into a romantic scene, twinkling with ersatz splendor, we might well miss the true beauty of the first Christmas. The fact is that the Son of God *gave up* his heavenly glory to experience our fallen humanity. We must keep that contrast sharp if we want to see his humility in all its beauty.

C. S. Lewis went so far as to describe the incarnation as an "irreverent doctrine"—irreverent because instead of protecting God the Son from our human troubles, this doctrine shows him entering in. Lewis pointed adoringly to this profound humility, which "decreed that God should become a baby at a peasant-woman's breast, and later an arrested field-preacher at the hands of the Roman police."[12] Jesus is beautiful in his humility.

The Beauty of Holiness

Jesus is also beautiful in his *holiness*. To be holy is to be set apart for God. Holiness stands for everything that is right and pure.

---

11 Thomas Dubay, *The Evidential Power of Beauty: Science and Theology Meet* (San Francisco: Ignatius, 1999), 307.
12 C. S. Lewis, introduction to J. B. Phillips, *Letters to Young Churches: A Translation of the New Testament Epistles* (London: Macmillan, 1947).

When the word is used for persons, it bears witness to their moral perfection.

Holiness is strongly associated with Jesus Christ, the sinless Son of God. Indeed, holiness inheres within his divine nature. Conceived by the Holy Spirit, Jesus was set apart for God even from before his birth. The angel Gabriel said to Mary, "The Holy Spirit will come upon you, and the power of the Most High will overshadow you; therefore the child to be born will be called holy—the Son of God" (Luke 1:35). Just as the beauty of the Spirit makes Jesus beautiful, so also the holiness of the Spirit makes him holy.

Given our Savior's divine conception by the Holy Spirit, it is not surprising that the word *holy* comes up frequently in the world's Christmas carols, such as "O Holy Night!"[13] It is there in "Silent Night," where our Savior is described as a "holy infant, so tender and mild."[14] Another carol begins by combining his humility with his holiness: "Infant holy, infant lowly, for His bed a cattle stall."[15] Long ago, the psalmist commanded us to "worship the LORD in the beauty of holiness" (Ps. 96:9 KJV). We do this every Christmas when we honor the Christ child for his pristine holiness.

We do not stop there, however. Jesus lived his whole life in holy obedience to the Father. Although he was a man among men, as the Son of God he was set apart from sinners. He was not simply born a holy child; he also lived a holy life. As we sing in another Christmas carol, "With the poor and mean and lowly / Lived on

---

13 Placide Cappeau, "O Holy Night" (1847). Public domain.

14 Joseph Mohr, "Silent Night" (1818). Public domain.

15 Edith M. G. Reed, "Infant Holy, Infant Lowly" (1921). Public domain.

earth our Savior holy."[16] All through his childhood, Jesus honored his parents with humble obedience (Luke 2:51). Then as he entered his public ministry, he never committed even one tiny little sin. Thus, the Scriptures praise our Savior for his holiness. The first Christians in Jerusalem called him God's "holy servant Jesus" (Acts 4:27, 30), "the Holy and Righteous One" (Acts 3:14). Even the demons acknowledged him as "the Holy One of God" (Mark 1:24).

In a word, Jesus is *holy*, and this is beautiful. When John said that he and others had seen the "glory as of the only Son" (John 1:14), he was referring in part to what he witnessed on the Mount of Transfiguration, when suddenly he saw Jesus radiate with the visible glory of God (Mark 9:2–13). Perhaps John also had in mind the seven signs he recorded in his Gospel—the signature miracles Jesus performed to reveal the glory of God. Maybe he also meant the beautiful way that Jesus treated other people, which is evident from every story that anyone ever told about him. The glory that John witnessed is especially apparent to anyone who looks at the life of Jesus and beholds the beauty of his holiness. Although he was tempted in every way, as we are, he lived completely without sin (Heb. 4:15; cf. 2 Cor. 5:21).

In our unholy and sinful condition, we can only admire the absolute purity of our Savior. In his book on seeing God's beauty in everyday life, Steve DeWitt invites us to consider the character of Jesus Christ and lays down this challenge:

Try to think of a moral or spiritual category in which He is not the highest expression ever. Think of His compassion, self-

16   Cecil Frances Alexander, "Once in Royal David's City" (1848). Public domain.

sacrifice, giving, love, and kindness. Think of an attribute that you wish was better represented in your life. Strength. Courage. Wisdom. Integrity. Leadership. Power. Humility. Jesus perfectly expresses it, doesn't He? He is the ultimate standard for every noble characteristic we admire.[17]

When we look at Jesus, therefore, we see the holiness of God in all its beauty. Thomas Dubay claims that for us simply to meet Jesus "as he was and is with open, unclouded eyes is to be struck with a self-validating luminosity. Indeed, he is the very radiancy of the Father's everlasting glory, and he shines by his own light."[18] If Jesus came to us as "the only Son from the Father" (John 1:14), then to see him is to see the Father (John 14:9). To see the Father, in turn, is to see the holiness of his divine nature, which is his essential beauty. When by the Spirit we see Jesus in his holiness, we behold the very brightness of God's beauty.

The Beauty of Sacrifice

In the person of Jesus Christ, we see the beauty of humility, the beauty of holiness, and also the beauty of *sacrifice*. The reason why the Son of God became a man was not only to live with us but also to die for us, "to give his life as a ransom for many" (Matt. 20:28).

Without getting too far ahead of the story, we notice hints of his coming sacrifice from the very beginning of the Gospels—shadows that fall across the pages of the story of the first Christmas. From the outset, we know that Jesus is the Savior;

17 Steve DeWitt, *Eyes Wide Open: Enjoying God in Everything* (Grand Rapids, MI: Credo, 2011), 104–5.
18 Dubay, *Evidential Power of Beauty*, 120.

this is what his name means (Matt. 1:21). This early in the story, we can hardly imagine how Jesus will bring salvation. Yet in telling us how "the Word became flesh and dwelt among us" (John 1:14), John makes sure to mention the sad and surprising fact that when Jesus came into the world, his own people did not receive him (John 1:11). Mary was told more explicitly that her son would be a sign that people opposed and that as a sword pierced him, it would also pierce her soul (Luke 2:35). The Gospels thus foreshadow the rejection and the crucifixion of Jesus Christ.

These hints from the incarnation narratives indicate that God the Son did not come in bodily form simply to look beautiful but to do something beautiful. To do this beautiful thing, he first had to enter fully into our humanity. The soulful tenor Roland Hayes—in his most famous rendition of a traditional spiritual—envisioned God the Son speaking to God the Father this way about the connection between his incarnation and his crucifixion:

> Prepare me one body,
> I'll go down, I'll go down.
> Prepare me one body like Man;
> I'll go down and die.

The early church theologian Athanasius explained the connection between Christmas and the atonement more complexly in his treatise *On the Incarnation*:

> The Word perceived that corruption could not be got rid of otherwise than through death; yet He Himself, as the Word,

being immortal and the Father's Son, was such as could not die. For this reason, therefore, He assumed a body capable of death, in order that it, through belonging to the Word Who is above all, might become in dying sufficient exchange for all, and, itself remaining incorruptible through His indwelling, might thereafter put an end to corruption for all others as well, by the grace of the resurrection. It was by surrendering to death the body which He had taken, as an offering and sacrifice free from every stain, that He forthwith abolished death for His human brethren by the offering of the equivalent.[19]

In saying that God the Son had to assume a mortal body to do his saving work, Athanasius was taking his cue from the letter to the Hebrews, which says that since God's "children share in flesh and blood," Jesus "himself likewise partook of the same things, that through death he might destroy the one who has the power of death, that is the devil" (Heb. 2:14). The incarnation was absolutely necessary for our salvation. The same humanity that sinned also had to suffer for sin. Only in this way could the punishment fit the crime. "Therefore," Hebrews goes on to say, Jesus "had to be made like his brothers in every respect, so that he might become a merciful and faithful high priest in the service of God, to make propitiation for the sins of the people" (Heb. 2:17). God became a man so that he could atone for humanity's sin.

This too is beautiful—this willing submission, this saving action, this loving sacrifice. In his unforgettable book *The Sound of Life's Unspeakable Beauty*, violin maker Martin Schleske recalls

---

19 Athanasius, *On the Incarnation: The Treatise "De incarnatione verbi Dei,"* Popular Patristics Series (Crestwood, NY: St. Vladimir's Seminary Press, 1996), 35.

attending a worship service in which a mentally disabled man approached the Lord's Table to receive his first Communion. The young man knew enough of the ways of this world that when the celebrant offered him bread and wine, he hesitated and asked a sensible question: "How much does it cost?" Without a moment's hesitation, the priest gave the best possible answer: "It's already been paid for."[20] This is beautiful—the free gift of grace through the costly offering of Christ's body and blood.

Behold His Beauty

See how beautiful Jesus is! As the Son of God, incarnate, Jesus Christ is the perfect embodiment of divine beauty—not merely in his physical form but in his entire person. Jesus shows us the beauty of God—body, soul, and spirit—in a way we never could have witnessed unless the Word became flesh. It is only by his coming into the world that we could ever know the beauty of a Savior. For all its splendor, creation never could have shown us the beauty of humility in the way that Jesus could or the beauty of an atoning sacrifice that truly takes away the sin of the world.

In and of itself, humanity never could have shown us this beauty either. We needed the God-man to show it to us: the beauty of salvation. We begin to see it in our Savior's humble incarnation and then even more in his holy life, sacrificial death, miraculous resurrection, triumphant ascension, and glorious return on the last of all days. Every moment in his saving work is a new display of divine beauty.

Will you receive this beautiful Savior?

20 Martin Schleske, *The Sound of Life's Unspeakable Beauty*, trans. Janet Gesme (Grand Rapids, MI: Eerdmans, 2020), 315–16.

Sadly, not everyone does receive Jesus. The Word became flesh and dwelt among us. And yet, John says, even his own people did not receive him. This is shocking! The true and radiant light of Jesus Christ came into the world—the world that he made in the first place—and "yet the world did not know him" (John 1:10). People did not perceive his holy beauty, and therefore they did not receive his offer of forgiveness or his free gift of eternal life.

Thankfully, there are people who *do* see his glory, as John did. When they see Jesus, they behold in him the beauty of the one and only, and he becomes the object of their holy desire. Too often we think of Jesus primarily in terms of what he can do for us rather than of who he is in himself as the one who deserves all affection and adoration. Dubay corrects our self-centered spirituality by writing about a teenage girl in Soviet Russia whose heart was transformed when she chanced upon a forbidden copy of the Gospel of Luke. To describe what happened when she met Jesus in its sacred pages, she simply said, "I fell in love with Him." The Russian girl essentially had the same experience as Agnes of Rome, from the third century, who joyfully declared, "I am espoused to him whom the angels serve; sun and moon stand in wonder at his beauty."[21]

We too may stand in wonder at the beauty of Jesus Christ. When we do this, we witness a beauty that is not merely rare but unique: the beauty of the Savior. We also open our hearts to greater experiences of beauty in the world that he not only made but entered to redeem. From now on, we see all the world's beauty in the light of his radiant glory.

---

21 Dubay, *Evidential Power of Beauty*, 308, 315.

He had no form or majesty that we should look at him,
  and no beauty that we should desire him.
He was despised and rejected by men,
  a man of sorrows and acquainted with grief;
and as one from whom men hide their faces
  he was despised, and we esteemed him not.

ISAIAH 53:2–3

The figure on the Cross, covered in blood and spittle,
has been made repulsive by torment. What we see,
nevertheless, is the supreme work of art. We see a divine
act that takes existing matter, the matter of history and
prophecy, and weaves it into a new design, a fulfillment
that could not have been expected or predicted but, seen
by those who have the eyes and ears for it, is perfect, as
though no stroke of the pen, no flick of the paint, no note
or chord, could be changed without diminishment.

STRATFORD CALDECOTT

7

That Old, Ugly Cross

The Beauty of the Crucifixion

WE START THIS CHAPTER with a seeming contradiction that poses a direct challenge to the thesis of this book. At the center of our beauty-loving God's perfect plan for making us beautiful is something so grotesque and so offensive that people cannot even bear to look: the God-damnable death that Jesus died on the cross. Wrestling with this paradox, however, brings healing to the soul.

So far, we have witnessed many beautiful things: the living God in his triune majesty, the created world in its variegated splendor, human beings in the divine image, human sexuality in its mysterious wonder. We have seen the Son of God come into the world as the morning star of the Father's glory—beautiful in his deity and humility. All along, we have hoped in the reality that through faith in Jesus Christ and by the transforming power of the Holy Spirit, beauty is the guaranteed destiny—both individually and communally—of the people of God.

Yet at the center of God's plan for the beautification of the cosmos is an act of appalling ugliness and degrading humiliation that nevertheless took place according to "the definite plan and foreknowledge of God" (Acts 2:23). I refer, of course, to the cross where Christ was crucified, as well as to what the Scripture says about the physical form of our Savior. If God is beautiful, if people made in his image are beautiful, and if the life of the Son he sent into the world is beautiful, then why does the Bible explicitly tell us that the Messiah, Jesus, was *not* beautiful? The prophet Isaiah could hardly be clearer on this point:

> He had no form or majesty that we should look at him,
>   and no beauty that we should desire him. (Isa. 53:2)

The promised Christ was unattractive in his appearance. Indeed, the prophet says that Jesus "grew up" this way (Isa. 53:2), which implies that our Savior was more homely than handsome. Certainly, in his sufferings and death, Jesus became so physically disfigured that he was socially rejected. The horror of his cross thus screams against every sensibility of the divine aesthetic. It was so hideous that even the Father (in a manner of speaking, during the dark hours that his Son bore the guilt of our sin) looked away. Nevertheless, the Bible still tells us to look to Jesus on the cross for our salvation (e.g., Heb. 12:2).

Here we confront the paradox of the crucifixion, which was *both* the ugliest sin ever committed *and* the most beautiful sacrifice ever given. When we look at "the Passion and crucifixion of the Lord of glory," writes Thomas Dubay, we witness "consummate splendor in monstrous horror." There "at one and the same time we find supremely horrific ugliness and supremely divine and loving beauty."[1] In this paradox we also find our salvation, for the crucifixion of the Christ was the ugly sin that alone had the power to make this world beautiful again.

Why So Ugly?

To understand this shocking paradox, it will help us if we linger at the foot of the cross. Before rushing on too quickly to Easter Sunday and the triumph of the resurrection, we need to take a closer, harder look at the sufferings of our Savior.

What they did—what *we* did—to Jesus was ugly. It was ugly to betray that innocent man with a Judas kiss, ugly to put him— wrongly—on ecclesiastical and political trial, ugly to parade false witnesses against him and condemn him to die for crimes he did not commit—crimes that were not even crimes at all. It was ugly to mock him royally for claiming to be the King, to crown him with bloody thorns, to beat him, strike him, and spit in his face. Ugly too were the nails that pierced his hands and his feet, the game of chance to steal his last garment, the dark insults hurled against him in his dying hours, and the absolute agony of gasping for every breath—naked and afraid—as his life bled away.

According to the prophet Isaiah, these travails were so repulsive that people could not bear to look but despised the crucified Christ by hiding their faces (Isa. 53:3). This prophecy is especially profound when we consider how much Isaiah said throughout his writings about beauty and splendor. Of all the prophets, he

---

1   Thomas Dubay, *The Evidential Power of Beauty: Science and Theology Meet* (San Francisco: Ignatius, 1999), 111, 310.

was the most sensitive to beauty as the destiny of the people of God (see Isa. 62:3). Yet when he came to the saving work of the suffering servant, Isaiah saw it as so ugly that he turned away.

How ugly was the cross? It was as ugly as what Jesus was dying to deal with—as ugly as sin and death.

When we consider carefully what Jesus was doing on that old, rugged cross, we can understand why it was so ugly. To atone for our transgressions, Jesus had to shoulder our guilty sins. The apostle Paul said it as plainly as he could when he wrote, "For our sake he made him to be sin who knew no sin, so that in him we might become the righteousness of God" (2 Cor. 5:21). Simply put, Jesus bore the ugliness of all our sin on the cross.

Again and again throughout this book we have come up against the same problem that we all struggle with every day of our lives: the problem of sin. Our beautiful God made this world beautiful and made us to be beautiful too. Yet sadly, we see signs of ugliness everywhere we look. In "A Brief for the Defense," the poet Jack Gilbert lamented,

> Sorrow everywhere. Slaughter everywhere. If babies
> are not starving someplace, they are starving
> somewhere else. With flies in their nostrils.[2]

The evils of a fallen world are not just somewhere "out there"; they are also right here, among us and inside us. We are not yet

2 Jack Gilbert, "A Brief for the Defense," in *Refusing Heaven: Poems*, by Jack Gilbert, copyright © 2005 by Jack Gilbert. Used by permission of Alfred A. Knopf, an imprint of Knopf Doubleday Publishing Group, a division of Penguin Random House LLC. All rights reserved.

the beautiful people—or the beautiful community—that God is calling us to become.

In the face of the world's unspeakable evil, how can we find any real hope that God will fulfill our destiny and make his world beautiful again?

In a strange way, we find the hope of beauty in the ignominy of the crucifixion. If anyone ever dared to enter the sorrows and struggles of a fallen world, it was Jesus of Nazareth. Reflecting on his own personal travails with physical disability, Andy Abernethy describes our Savior as "a spectacle of deformity, paraded to Calvary. Suffering, deformed, and disabled. Like me. Like millions of others. He can relate; he became what I am."[3]

We can go further and dare to say that the cross *had* to be as ugly as it was in order to deal with the awful sin and guilt that it was destined to address. In a strange way, the ugliness of the cross gives us hope, therefore, because it shows that Jesus endured and ultimately conquered the worst problems in the world: injustice, hatred, abuse, and every transgression that we too have committed against the holiness of God.

Sometimes we wonder whether it is really possible for every wrong to be made right. Then we look at the cross—at the bullying, the torture, the humiliation, and the degradation—and we are able to say, "Yes, Jesus the Christ *has* entered *fully* into humanity's suffering and into *my* suffering because of sin." He did not save the world in the perfection of health and strength, in a body impervious to pain; Jesus did it in a body that was broken for sinners, suffering to his very soul for the sins of the world. As John Calvin

---

3 Andrew Abernethy, "Why Matthew's Disability in *The Chosen* Matters," The Gospel Coalition, May 7, 2021, https://www.thegospelcoalition.org/.

put it, "clothed with our flesh," Christ "offered as a sacrifice the flesh he received from us, that he might wipe out our guilt by his act of expiation and appease the Father's righteous wrath."[4]

Jesus died to bear our sin. He also died to put death to death. "The Son who is risen," writes Jeremy Begbie, is "the Son who was given up to the corrupting forces of sin and death afflicting creation."[5] This too was totally necessary—that in order to deal with death, our Savior had to suffer death's pain. Maybe Athanasius said it best in his famous treatise on the incarnation:

> The death of all was consummated in the Lord's body; yet, because the Word was in it, death and corruption were in the same act utterly abolished. Death there had to be, and death for all, so that the due of all might be paid. Wherefore, the Word, as I said, being Himself incapable of death, assumed a mortal body, that He might offer it as His own in place of all, and suffering for the sake of all through His union with it, "might bring to nought Him that had the power of death, that is, the devil, and might deliver them who all their lifetime were enslaved by the fear of death."[6]

Here again we see why the cross had to be so ugly. Death is an affront to the life of God, so dealing with death was ugly too.

4   John Calvin, *Institutes of the Christian Religion*, trans. Ford Lewis Battles, 2 vols., Library of Christian Classics 20–21 (Philadelphia: Westminster, 1960), 2.12.3.

5   Jeremy S. Begbie, "Beauty, Sentimentality and the Arts," in *The Beauty of God: Theology and the Arts*, ed. Daniel J. Treier, Mark Husbands, and Roger Lundin (Downers Grove, IL: IVP Academic, 2007), 64.

6   Athanasius, *On the Incarnation: The Treatise "De incarnatione verbi Dei,"* Popular Patristics Series (Crestwood, NY: St. Vladimir's Seminary Press, 1996), 49.

In death, said Melito of Sardis, "the beautiful body" that "once fitted beautifully" has been "split apart."[7] We see this horrific loss of beauty at Calvary. Bleeding from his extremities, with his chest collapsed, the crucified Christ put death on display in all its horror. Now we know—really know—that sin and death and every evil have found their adequate answer.

If we could bear to gaze on the fatal torture of the innocent one, then we might think that somehow his sufferings and death fell short of what was truly demanded to carry away our sin, do away with death, and wipe away every evil. But in fact, we *do* feel compelled to turn away. "Surely he *has* borne our griefs / and carried our sorrows" (Isa. 53:4). Indeed, "he *was* pierced for our transgressions" and "crushed for our iniquities" (Isa. 53:5). Truly, "the Lord *has* laid on him / the iniquity of us all" (Isa. 53:6). We know all this because Isaiah also said that "as one from whom men hide their faces / he was despised, and we esteemed him not" (Isa. 53:3). We cannot bear to look at the crucifixion any more than we can bear to look at the worst sins and most painful sorrows in the world—or to look inside and see the darkness of our own depravity. The old, ugly cross therefore serves as a proof that Jesus did what he meant to do and put an end to all our sin.

How So Beautiful?

In a strange way, the cross was also surprisingly beautiful, which brings us to the other side of a strange paradox: as ugly as it had to be to do what it was designed to do, the cross was also part of God's greatest masterpiece—the most beautiful sacrifice that

7   Melito of Sardis, quoted in Nancy Pearcey, *Love Thy Body: Answering Hard Questions about Life and Sexuality* (Grand Rapids, MI: Baker, 2018), 38.

anyone has ever made. Of all the places where "the glory of God shines," wrote John Calvin, "nowhere has it shone more brightly than in the cross."[8]

Where, specifically, does its beauty lie? No matter how many golden crosses people wear or great works of art take the crucifixion as their grand theme, the beauty of the cross is not physical or visual but spiritual and eschatological. The crucifixion is beautiful because of what it means for our redemption and the eternal healing of every wound in our sin-wrecked souls.

The cross is beautiful as the fulfillment of ancient prophecy. According to Moses and the Prophets—the Scriptures of the Old Testament—it was necessary for the Christ to suffer unto death for the salvation of his people (Luke 24:25–27; cf. Mark 8:31). Isaiah 53 is perhaps the clearest of these prophecies, but it is not the only one. It was also said that the Savior would be betrayed by someone who shared his bread (Ps. 41:9), that he would be sold for thirty pieces of silver (Zech. 11:12), that he would feel forsaken by God (Ps. 22:7–8), that he would be as thirsty as the dust (Ps. 22:15), that his enemies would strip away his clothes (Ps. 22:17–18), and that he would remove our iniquity in a single day (Zech. 3:9). Therefore, when we see Jesus on the cross, we see the beautiful fulfillment of God's plan for our redemption— a plan so old that the Bible calls Jesus "the Lamb who was slain from the creation of the world" (Rev. 13:8 NIV; cf. Titus 1:1–2; 1 Pet. 1:18–21). The story of our salvation itself is a work of art, with the cross at its center.

---

8   John Calvin, *Commentary on the Gospel of John*, quoted in Jonathan King, *The Beauty of the Lord: Theology as Aesthetics*, Studies in Historical and Systematic Theology (Bellingham, WA: Lexham, 2018), 221.

The cross is beautiful as a sacrifice too. Linguists tell us that the Japanese word for beauty includes the concept of sacrifice. For the contemporary Japanese American artist Makoto Fujimura, this connection helps explain why he must crush minerals to produce the colors that make his paintings so beautiful:

> The Japanese ideogram for beauty is built with two Chinese characters, "sheep" and "great." Apparently, in China, beauty was a "fat (great) sheep." But in Japan, with the contribution of Sen-no-Rikyu and others, this word for beauty became refined and abstract. Beauty became associated with death and its sorrow. "Mono-no-aware," an expression that captures the sentiment of sorrow (literally, "sorrow of things"), points to the notion of beauty as sacrifice. To enjoy the feast at a banquet, the sheep must be sacrificed. Autumn leaves are most beautiful and bright as they are distressed with their impending death. The minerals I use must be pulverized to bring out their true beauty.[9]

Maybe this is always true, that there is no beauty without sacrifice, that the artist must always pay a costly price to produce a work of beauty. Certainly, we see this on the cross, where the Son of God died in our place and gave himself up as our substitute. There is beauty in the offering when one life is given so that other lives are gained.

Jesus did this all for love, which is another reason why his cross is so beautiful. His crucifixion demonstrates divine love for fallen humanity. "The cruciform of Christ on the cross," writes Jonathan

9   Makoto Fujimura, "True Beauty," *Makoto Fujimura*, May 3, 2001, https://makoto fujimura.com/.

King, "magnifies the beauty of the glory of God's self-giving love."[10] Jesus said, "Greater love has no one than this, that someone lay down his life for his friends" (John 15:13). By this standard, what he did on the cross is the greatest love of all—the proof that "God so loved the world" (John 3:16). And not just the world in general: Jesus died for us as much as he died for anyone, proving that he loves us as much as he loves anyone. Thomas Dubay writes,

> Far, far beyond all created beauties, breathtaking as we have seen them to be, is the divine glory that shines out from this unsurpassable love found in the torture of Holy Week: Perfection himself whipped to blood, crowned with thorns, mocked, spit upon, ridiculed, nailed, pierced—all because he loves you and me, who have in return sinned against him.[11]

This is not to say that what Jesus suffered was beautiful in and of itself. On the contrary, the cross is an ugly obscenity. Yet our Savior's sufferings remain forever a beautiful demonstration of his love. Wrestling with the paradox of the ugly-beautiful cross, Jeremy Begbie clarifies what he does and does not mean when he describes the cross as a beautiful demonstration of our Savior's love:

> This is emphatically *not* to say that the crucifixion as an event of torture and death is really beautiful and not ugly, if only we would change our perspective. . . . But it is to say that in and through this particular torture, crucifixion and death, God's

10 King, *Beauty of the Lord*, 225.
11 Dubay, *Evidential Power of Beauty*, 311.

love is displayed at its most potent. The "form" of beauty here is the radiant, splendid form of God's self-giving love.[12]

The results are beautiful too—what Jesus lovingly accomplished for us through the work he finished on the cross. The cross means that we have forgiveness—the pardon of all our sins. It means we have hope—the hope of healing, happiness, and eternal life with God, with final justice for every wrong that has ever been done. It means we have a Savior who is able to sympathize with our sorrows because he suffered in all the ways that we suffer, even unto death. It means there is beauty in our destiny too, for "the transfiguring power of supernatural beauty to change evil to good, suffering to delight, ugliness to splendor is seen on the hill of Calvary."[13]

Augustine wrestled openly with this paradox in one of his sermons. "Now I am going to make a bold statement," he said to his congregation, doubtless arousing the curiosity of even his sleepiest parishioners. Referring to the church of Jesus Christ, Augustine said, "To render her beautiful he loved her even when she was ugly." Then he proceeded to make a still more daring assertion: "To make her beautiful he became ugly himself." Lest this seem unduly irreverent, the bishop defended his claim: "That would not have been a fitting statement to make in the presence of people who love him, but for the fact that Scripture bore witness to it before I did."[14]

---

12 Begbie, "Beauty, Sentimentality and the Arts," 63.

13 Dubay, *Evidential Power of Beauty*, 110.

14 Augustine, quoted in Jason Byassee, *Psalms 101–150*, Brazos Theological Commentary on the Bible (Grand Rapids, MI: Brazos, 2018), 26.

To understand this true biblical paradox and to receive and indeed to become the beauty that God has promised in his word, we must not turn away from the cross but look toward it. Commenting specifically on Isaiah 53, the Swiss theologian Karl Barth wrote, "If the beauty of Christ is sought in a glorious Christ who is not the crucified, the search will always be in vain."[15] But when we look to the crucified Lord Jesus Christ, we see the beauty of what he has done for our salvation. The gospel is beautiful!

The Beauty Marks of the Risen Christ

Paradoxically, the cross on which Jesus died is *both* ugly *and* beautiful—physically ugly and spiritually beautiful. It is also beautiful *eschatologically*, which is a further mystery. After Jesus died, he also came back to life. When we view his crucifixion in the light of the empty tomb, we see evidence of its everlasting beauty in the physical body of the risen Christ. This is because our Savior's glorified resurrection body now bears and will forever bear beauty marks from the cross.

We know from the story of doubting (and eventually believing!) Thomas that Jesus still had the scars to prove that he was crucified. Thomas had told his fellow disciples—perhaps quite reasonably—that he would not believe in the resurrection until he could evaluate the evidence for himself. "Unless I see in his hands the mark of the nails," he said, "and place my finger into the mark of the nails, and place my hand into his side, I will never believe" (John 20:25). Well, Thomas did see for himself, and when he saw, he believed. One look at the body of the risen

15 Karl Barth, *Church Dogmatics*, 2.1:661, 665, quoted in Patrick Sherry, *Spirit and Beauty: An Introduction to Theological Aesthetics*, 2nd ed. (London: SCM, 2002), 74.

Christ was all it took for him to know for certain that Jesus is not dead but alive.

For endless ages, Jesus will continue to bear the scars of his suffering as the proof of our salvation—beautiful, healed, glorified scars. His glorious body will remind us what he endured for our salvation and display the proof that he has conquered sin and death, our "last enemy" (1 Cor. 15:26). Matthew Bridges expressed this truth in one of the most profound lyrics ever penned. In his triumphant hymn "Crown Him with Many Crowns," Bridges described the scars of our Savior as "rich wounds yet visible above in beauty glorified."[16] Irwyn Ince explains the significance of these words:

> The marks of human history—human sinfulness, depravity, and injustice—are indelibly inscribed upon the flesh of the resurrected Lord, carried into the life of the new creation by the Spirit, and transfigured. These marks in no way tarnish the glory of the new creation, but rather "those wounds, yet visible above" are "in beauty glorified."[17]

We began this book by talking about the beatific vision—the glorious destiny of every believer to see the indescribably beautiful glory of God in the face of Jesus Christ. His face, however, is not the only place we will look to see his beauty. We will also see it in his hands, his feet, and his side. This hope is expressed beautifully in the final, triumphant stanza of "The Sands of Time

16 Matthew Bridges, "Crown Him with Many Crowns" (1915). Public domain.
17 Irwyn Ince, *The Beautiful Community: Unity, Diversity, and the Church at Its Best* (Downers Grove, IL: InterVarsity Press, 2020), 29.

Are Sinking"—a hymn by Anne Ross Cousin that for decades was among the most popular in America:

> The Bride eyes not her garments
> But her dear Bridegroom's face;
> I will not gaze at glory
> But on my King of grace.
> Not at the crown He giveth
> But on His pierced hand:
> The Lamb is all the glory
> Of Immanuel's land.[18]

When we gaze not only on our Savior's radiant face but also on his wounded hands—now healed—we see for ourselves what the artist Bruce Herman has described as the "new form of beauty" that God inaugurated when Jesus ascended to "heaven bearing the marks of earthly pain." In this "new aesthetic," as Herman calls it, "the marks of Christ's resurrected body" that "memorialize suffering" also "move beyond it to redemption, healing and eternity."[19]

Consider what this new form of beauty—one that "leaves room for scars"[20]—must mean for our own pains and sorrows. Simply put, God is too good an artist to leave all the ugliness as it is. What he did for the body of his Son beyond the grave is the same thing he will do for everyone who belongs to his body, the church. By "engaging directly with the world's wounded and deformed

18 Anne Ross Cousin, "The Sands of Time Are Sinking" (1857). Public domain.

19 Bruce Herman, "Wounds and Beauty," in Treier, Husbands, and Lundin, *Beauty of God*, 111, 118.

20 Ince, *Beautiful Community*, 29.

beauty," writes Jeremy Begbie, "the incarnate Son, crucified, risen and now exalted," has reached "the ultimate measure of created beauty" and has given us "an anticipation of God's re-creation of the world's beauty," including our own re-created beauty.[21] As surely as he beautified and glorified his beloved Son, our loving Father will mend what is broken. He will heal what is wounded. He will raise what is dead. He will do what he promised and make "everything beautiful in its time" (Eccl. 3:11).

Standing on this side of eternity, still enduring the woes of a fallen and wounded world, the beauty of the ugly cross remains a strange paradox for us. But one day—when we are finally beautified—it will all make perfect sense. Our bodies will bear witness to the truth of a memorable epigram from Augustine: "He hung on the cross deformed, but his deformity is our beauty."[22]

---

21 Begbie, "Beauty, Sentimentality and the Arts," 64.
22 Augustine, quoted in Sherry, *Spirit and Beauty*, 74.

*There is neither Jew nor Greek, there is neither
slave nor free, there is no male and female,
for you are all one in Christ Jesus.*

GALATIANS 3:28

*When the fear and the pride go away and all we see is the
beauty of what He's done—then we can love Him just
because He's beautiful. Because of all He's given me, I don't
have to do anything to get anything; I just want Him.
I can love the poor for the poor's sake. I can love God for
God's sake—that's the beauty that will change your heart.
That's the beauty that will get you out of yourself forever.*

TIM KELLER

8

Beautiful Community

The Beauty of Christ's Bride

THE LAUSANNE MOVEMENT pursues this world-changing vision: "The gospel for every person, disciple-making churches for every people and place, Christ-like leaders for every church and sector, and kingdom impact in every sphere of society."[1]

In 2016 the artist Bryn Gillette received a commission to create four paintings based on these four pillars of Lausanne's mission. To illustrate *an evangelical church for every community*, Gillette produced a stunning work of art. Its central image is a tall, beautiful woman depicted against a night sky illuminated with countless stars, giving her a planetary scale. Her skin is dark to represent the global church, which today has a majority of black and brown faces. In her hand she holds the bright light of the gospel. Streaming from her long blue gown are people of every

[1] Lausanne Movement, "About the Movement," accessed November 16, 2022, https://lausanne.org.

tribe, every tongue, and every nation. The woman represents the beautiful bride of Christ, glorious in her perfection.

To see the image of this transcendent bride is to be captivated by a vision of what God's people can and will become. By the grace of God, beauty is our destiny! We need this vision because in the present time, we are living a different reality. The church we see is not as beautiful as this painting—not as fully global, as genuinely diverse, as truly unified, as clearly illuminated by the gospel, or as radiant in its witness. These shortcomings cause us to long for the day when the people of God will finally look as beautiful as our Savior does.

Born Again to Be Beautiful

It may be helpful to stop here and summarize again what we have learned so far in our consideration of beauty. We have seen that God is beautiful in his triunity. His being is beauty itself—Father, Son, and Holy Spirit. We have seen that our beautiful God created a beautiful universe, including the beautiful men and women that he made in his divine image. We have also seen how beautiful it can be when a man and a woman become one flesh. Perhaps most importantly, we have seen that to redeem his broken yet beautiful people, God sent his Son into the world to suffer and die on the ugly cross of sin and shame before rising again in radiant glory—our beautiful Savior.

Now we widen our perspective to witness the beauty of the community that Jesus died to save and rescued from the grave. The goal of God's kingdom is not simply to redeem individual believers but to create a new humanity in Jesus Christ—what the New Testament simply calls "the church." "We are being shaped and formed into a new in-group," writes Irwyn Ince. "God isn't just making a new me, he's making a new *we*."[2]

As soon as that community began to come to life—immediately following the ascension of Jesus Christ and the incoming of the Holy Spirit—people started to see its beauty. Fifty days after Jesus returned to heaven, on the day of Pentecost, the power of the Holy Spirit was poured out on the early church. On that very first day, through the preaching of Peter and the other apostles, three thousand people put their personal trust in Jesus. They were people "from every nation under heaven" (Acts 2:5). All of them heard the gospel in their own language: "Parthians and Medes and Elamites and residents of Mesopotamia, Judea and Cappadocia, Pontus and Asia, Phrygia and Pamphylia, Egypt and the parts of Libya belonging to Cyrene, and visitors from Rome, both Jews and proselytes, Cretans and Arabians" (Acts 2:9–11). All these people from all these places repented of their sins and believed the gospel. It must have been beautiful to see them baptized—people from every background washed clean by the life-saving blood of Jesus Christ.

They were also beautiful in their spiritual unity. The book of Acts goes on to provide a remarkable description of their shared commitment to the word of God, to loving fellowship, to the sacrament of the Lord's Supper, to worship and prayer, to deeds of mercy, and to giving generously to brothers and sisters in need:

And they devoted themselves to the apostles' teaching and the fellowship, to the breaking of bread and the prayers. And

2   Irwyn Ince, *The Beautiful Community: Unity, Diversity, and the Church at Its Best* (Downers Grove, IL: InterVarsity Press, 2020), 126, 143.

awe came upon every soul, and many wonders and signs were being done through the apostles. And all who believed were together and had all things in common. And they were selling their possessions and belongings and distributing the proceeds to all, as any had need. And day by day, attending the temple together and breaking bread in their homes, they received their food with glad and generous hearts, praising God and having favor with all the people. And the Lord added to their number day by day those who were being saved. (Acts 2:42–47)

Have you ever belonged to a church this diverse, this united, and this effective at reaching the lost for Jesus Christ? Such a congregation is much rarer than it ought to be. Yet the New Testament does not present the apostolic church as something unusual; rather, it regards becoming a beautiful community as the ordinary experience of the people of God.

This does not mean that the first Christians never had any problems, and it certainly does not mean that the church in the world is as beautiful today as it should be. Yet the Holy Spirit does bring inherent splendor to the church of Jesus Christ—what Ince calls "the beautiful community." The generosity of the first Christians was beautiful: they gave of themselves to one another. Their intercultural diversity and harmony were beautiful: only in the church could all these people groups come together. Their witness was beautiful: non-Christians were deeply attracted to the loving community they could find only in the church, with the result that every day some of them gave their lives to Jesus Christ.

At the center of it all was the Son of God, the church's Savior and Lord. Here is how Ince describes the beautifully diverse, newly unified community that God was creating for the world, starting in Jerusalem:

> The Spirit of God worked to press the people of God into the new normal of having Jesus Christ at the center of their identity. . . . This did not mean that ethnic identities were no longer apparent or significant. . . . Instead, those who belonged to Christ were to understand their ethnic identity as subservient to their identity in Christ.[3]

God always intended this new normal—a multiethnic multitude bearing united witness to Jesus Christ—to become our eternal normal. Promises about this beautiful community go back at least as far as Abraham. Remember what God said to that patriarch on a starry night: "I will make of you a great nation, . . . and in you all the families of the earth shall be blessed" (Gen. 12:2–3). We can go back even further, however, to the garden of Eden. There God made a man and a woman in his own beautiful image and told them to fill the earth with their beloved children. While each of us individually embodies the divine image, God's purpose in creating human beings was also for us to bear his image in the world *together*—not solely as individuals or only as ethnicities or merely as cultures but corporately as one new worldwide humanity in Jesus Christ.

Together, we bear the image of God. Here is how the Dutch theologian Herman Bavinck explained God's beautiful plan:

---

3   Ince, *Beautiful Community*, 97.

The image of God . . . is much too rich for it to be fully real-ized in a single human being, however richly gifted that human being may be. . . . Only humanity in its entirety—as one complete organism, summed up under a single head, spread out over the whole earth, as prophet proclaiming the truth of God, as priest dedicating itself to God, as ruler controlling the earth and the whole of creation—only it is the fully finished image, the most telling and striking likeness of God.[4]

Our collective calling to represent the image of God together means that all the beauty we have considered so far in this book culminates in—of all places—the church of Jesus Christ. In this splendid community, we are meant to see the beauty of God's image, the beauty of embodied humanity, and the beauty of the Savior who came to make us one—all brought together by the beautifying power of God the Holy Spirit.

To say this another way, the church is the outworking of God's triune beauty. There is only one God, yet there is diversity as well as unity within and among the three persons of the Trinity. According to Bavinck, the Trinity "reveals God to us as the fullness of being, the true life, eternal beauty. In God, too, there is unity in diversity, diversity in unity."[5] Simply put, God *is* beautiful community, and we, in turn, are called to embody that beauty:

God is the apex of unchanging beauty as Father, Son, and Holy Spirit in eternally existent, mutually glorifying, loving, honor-ing, and supporting diverse community. As his people, when

4 Herman Bavinck, quoted in Ince, *Beautiful Community*, 56.
5 Bavinck, quoted in Ince, *Beautiful Community*, 12.

we are mutually glorifying, speaking, and acting in ways that enhance the reputations of one another, striving to bring praise and honor to others, and submit to one another—especially across lines of difference—we are imaging God's beauty.[6]

Given this beautiful and diversely unified calling, it is not surprising that many (if not all) of the metaphors that the New Testament authors use to describe the church are images of surpassing beauty. John compares the new people of God to a beautiful vine—green, fruitful, abundant (John 15:1–17; cf. Isa. 4:2–6). Peter compares us to a beautiful temple, in which every stone is alive to God (1 Pet. 2:4–10; cf. Pss. 48:2; 96:6). Paul draws an analogy to the human body, with every part working together in beautiful harmony (1 Cor. 12:12–17). Most beautiful of all, the church is like a bride on her wedding day—perfectly glorious (Eph. 5:25–32; Rev. 21:2; cf. Ps. 45:11). When the world looks at the church, therefore, it is meant to witness the living and supernatural beauty of God.

Ugly Exclusion

Why, then, are we so ugly? Everywhere we look, we catch glimpses of the beauty that our Creator has put into the world—his divine beauty displayed in creation and reflected in the people he saved. But we also see the deformity of sin wherever we look, and sometimes the church looks like the ugliest community in the world. If we were created, redeemed, and destined to be beautiful, then why are we so unattractive?

6   Ince, *Beautiful Community*, 55.

Sadly, this ugliness was apparent already in the time of Christ. Jesus reserved some of his harshest criticisms for religious leaders who claimed to follow God yet actually led people astray by their hypocrisy. They were "serpents" (Matt. 23:33), he said— "whitewashed tombs" (Matt. 23:27), "blind guides" (Matt. 15:14) that turned their followers into children of hell (Matt. 23:13). Judging by these analogies, there was nothing beautiful about them.

We find the same flaws in the early church. As we read the New Testament Epistles, we encounter two main themes. One is the beauty of Jesus Christ in his atoning death, triumphant resurrection, and glorious ascension to heaven. The other is the ugliness of the Christian community in its ungodliness. The long lists of vices that we find in the epistles of Paul, for example (Gal. 5:19–21; 2 Tim. 3:2–5), were not hypotheticals for the early church; they were discouraging everyday realities.

The picture of the church we get at the end of Acts 2 is beautiful: charity, unity, generosity. By the time we get to Acts 6, however, we see clear signs of racial division. The majority Jewish Christians were overlooking the minority Greek Christians in the daily distribution of food for lonely widows and hungry orphans. Praise God, our fathers and mothers in the faith were able to work things out in a way that shared leadership across ethnic lines and restored spiritual harmony (Acts 6:1–7). But there are racial and social dimensions to almost every church conflict that we read about in the rest of the New Testament. Paul told the Galatians that in Jesus Christ "there is neither Jew nor Greek, there is neither slave nor free, there is no male and female" (Gal. 3:28) because he knew that divisions caused by race, class, and gender posed some of the biggest threats to the witness of the church.

Is anything uglier than disunity? Some of the strongest warnings in the New Testament relate to actions and attitudes that divide the church. Yes, we are warned about sins like idolatry and sexual immorality. But we are also warned about discord, slander, jealousy, backbiting, and a long list of other divisive habits that destroy Christian fellowship. On the night that he was betrayed, as Jesus prayed over his disciples, his main concern was for us to become one—for us to have the same essential unity that the Father has with the Son (John 17:20–21). Unity was our Savior's priority. Yet as we read the New Testament—and consider our own painful experience of living in Christian community—sometimes we almost wonder whether the Holy Spirit was listening.

Where is the beautiful church that our Savior promised and prayed for? When the prophet Jeremiah mourned for a fallen Jerusalem, he asked,

> Is this the city that was called
> the perfection of beauty? (Lam. 2:15)

The chasm between the prophet's lived experience and God's beautiful promise was so vast that it left him looking for answers. We too are looking for answers. Sadly, we wonder, Why are God's people so divided—by theological discord, gender conflict, racial strife, cultural confusion, and political disunity?

These questions matter because the church is meant to be the beautiful body of Christ. Throughout this book we have lamented the ugliness that sin has brought into the world. Here the cost of broken beauty is perhaps most tragic. We cannot simply go around and say, "I know the church looks like a mess sometimes, but Jesus never fails." This is not how evangelism is supposed to work. Instead, we are meant to make Jesus visible to the world as the beautiful embodiment of his life-giving grace. How will the world see how beautiful Jesus is unless the community that bears his name also bears witness to his beauty?

When we tear one another down, when we bear false witness against our neighbors to prove our point, when we perpetuate negative stereotypes about people from other ethnic backgrounds, when we belittle the gifts of the opposite gender, when we exclude people who come from other social classes, when we disparage dissenting voices—we no longer bear witness to the beauty of the gospel in ways the Holy Spirit can use to bring people to Christ.

Becoming More Beautiful

Today many young adults—including many who grew up in Christian families—are turning away from Christ. Is it possible that they are changing spiritual directions because they have never seen the kind of Christianity we read about in the book of Acts? If so, then what would it take for us to become a church that has the beauty to draw people to Jesus?

The Holy Spirit has a sanctifying—that is, beautifying—work of grace to do in our Christian communities. To that end, the Spirit is calling us to pursue the practices our fathers and mothers in the faith put on display for us in Acts 2.

Practice Hospitality

We all have our preferences, and one of our preferences is to spend most of our time with people who are more like us. The early church was challenged to welcome people who were *not* like them. Not only in Jerusalem but also in Antioch and throughout Asia Minor, Jews and Gentiles worshiped together in the same congregations. So did people from many different nations. The way they connected was by welcoming one another into their most personal spaces: their homes. Practicing such hospitality is especially incumbent on people from the majority culture (whoever they happen to be in a particular context) because they are the most at home already.

The goal of our hospitality goes beyond simply making others feel welcome to helping them feel truly at home. Here it may be helpful for us to ask ourselves some hard questions about which people we are making time for, building new relationships with, welcoming into our personal space, and most of all treating as truly loved and respected equals. For this is what beloved community requires, as Ince explains:

> In order to be in community, we have to experience belonging, a sense of being at home. More expressly, belonging is an individual's community experience of being at home among friends as a *co-owner* and *creator* of that community. It includes an individual's sense of being rightly placed in a specific community and feeling welcomed, valued, comfortable, or safe.[7]

Give Generously

Hospitality is one form of generosity, in which we give our time, our space, and ourselves to care for the needs of our guests. But the first Christians in Jerusalem and elsewhere did more than open their homes; they also opened their purses. When they saw a need,

---

7 Ince, *Beautiful Community*, 99.

they met it. Thus, in those days it was common for Christians to sell their property and their possessions in order to have more money to give to the poor, support their churches, and provide for missionaries. They gave from their substance, not simply their excess. They did this because the Holy Spirit had given them "generous hearts" (Acts 2:46).

The Holy Spirit wants to make our hearts beautiful too. In a world that is broken by sin, we have so many opportunities to house refugees, support adoption, care for the incarcerated, feed the homeless, train the jobless, and advance the worldwide proclamation of the gospel. Christians who get in the habit of giving, even in small ways, enjoy it so much that they start looking for ways to give even more. In God's economy there is always joyful spiritual abundance for those who give.

Do Justice

People who do justice are also blessed. Our righteous God—the God who executed justice at the cross for the cause of mercy and has promised a day of judgment to settle accounts for all wrongs—calls us to be righteous too, and this includes doing right by our brothers and sisters in Christ.

As we have seen, there was a notable example of rectifying a wrong at the first church in Jerusalem, where the minority Greeks were getting overlooked in the daily distribution of food for the hungry. Ironically, this disparity meant that the church was being unjust in the way it was showing mercy! When Greek believers came forward to share their concerns about inequity, something remarkable happened: leaders from the majority community listened, actually listened. They recognized that the continued unity of their community depended on first addressing the cause of division. Rather than dismissing the concern or trying to defend themselves by saying that they did not mean to discriminate, they humbly admitted that there was a problem. They also came up with a practical solution: they shared leadership by putting Greek-speaking leaders in charge of the church's mercy ministry.

Doing justice often starts with truly listening—not minimizing what people are feeling or denying that there is a problem but believing what is said and then addressing it in a God-honoring way. When we prefer one another and defer to one another, we imitate God's triune love, in which each person of the Trinity honors the others. We also come to see the beauty in one another, which leads to greater respect, stronger relationships, and deeper *shalom*. These happy results confirm Elaine Scarry's bold claim that "beauty, far from contributing to social injustice . . . or even remaining neutral to injustice as an innocent bystander, actually assists us in the work of addressing injustice."[8]

Pursue Reconciliation

For our community to be restored, we must move toward one another. God's purpose in Jesus Christ is to break down our walls of hostility and reconcile us by making us one (see Eph. 2:11–16). We are called to practice what Jarvis Williams aptly calls "redemptive kingdom diversity."[9]

---

8 Elaine Scarry, *On Beauty and Being Just* (Princeton, NJ: Princeton University Press, 1999), 62.

9 Jarvis J. Williams, *Redemptive Kingdom Diversity: A Biblical Theology of the People of God* (Grand Rapids, MI: Baker, 2021). See especially the concluding chapter, "The People of God and Orthopraxy," 152–89.

Reconciliation is all too rare, but it is beautiful when it happens. Christian filmmaker Joonhee Park documented one small but striking example when he visited Rwanda and photographed Narcisse and Evariste. The two men were neighbors. During the violent tribal conflict between the Hutus and the Tutsis in 1994, Evariste was part of a mob that clubbed Narcisse's mother to death. When the war was finally over, he rightly assumed that his enemy would seek revenge. Yet as much as he feared for his life, Evariste also knew that it was right to confess his sins, so he went to Narcisse and asked forgiveness. This was such a costly request that they did not reconcile right away. In fact, at the time, Narcisse was devising a plan to kill Evariste and his entire family. But the Holy Spirit touched Narcisse's heart and led him to Christ. God's reconciling Spirit also inspired Evariste to ask forgiveness again and healed their relationship. Narcisse told Evariste, "I forgive you today more than I forgave you before." In Park's beautiful photographs of the two men, it is difficult if not impossible to tell who is the victim and who is the perpetrator because they have become true brothers.

If two such sworn enemies can be reconciled to one another, then by God's grace our own deep divisions can be healed as well. Our calling is to reach out in reliance on the reconciling grace of God the Holy Spirit.

Live in Christian Unity

Whenever the New Testament highlights the diversity of the church—and wrestles with the painful divisions we often experience—it always works from the bedrock assumption of our unity in Jesus Christ. We see a striking example of this when believers in

Christ first moved to Antioch. The citizens there needed a name to describe the remarkable new religious community that had come to their city, so they called them "Christians" (Acts 11:26). This new name for believers in Jesus expressed their core identity and common unity. Although diverse in their backgrounds, occupations, and ethnicities, they all belonged to Christ and found their primary identity in him.

Christian unity is not so much an aspiration as it is a presupposition. Because of Christ's death and resurrection and by the indwelling work of his Spirit, we are one in Jesus Christ. No other basis for unity will suffice; he alone "is able to bear the weight of the center."[10] Our unity in Christ is a fact, despite the way that things sometimes appear. God's ever-listening Holy Spirit *has* answered and will continue to answer the great prayer of Jesus Christ: that we may be one as the Father and Son are one (John 17:11).

Now it is up to us to live out the common unity that the Spirit has given us. Surprisingly enough, one of the most important ways we practice that unity is by celebrating our diversity! "Diversity is neither a limitation on nor a correction of unity," says Raniero Cantalamessa, "but the only way to realize it."[11] When the things that make us different become reasons for celebration rather than division, then our common unity is strengthened.

Only selfless love can bind us together in such perfect harmony (Col. 3:14). Violin maker Martin Schleske finds apt illustrations for this union in the process of crafting a new instrument. As

10   Ince, *Beautiful Community*, 96–97.
11   Raniero Cantalamessa, *Die Kirche lieben*, quoted in Martin Schleske, *The Sound of Life's Unspeakable Beauty*, trans. Janet Gesme (Grand Rapids, MI: Eerdmans, 2020), 302.

he strives to produce both warmth and brilliance in the tonal colors of a violin, he knows that "only in the space of harmonious opposites can sound and beauty expand."[12] Schleske also pursues beauty in the varnish he applies to stringed instruments as the last step in their construction. The lustrous varnish is not a simple substance but a carefully mixed combination of various oils and resins. Observing a similar amalgamation in the Christian community, he writes, "The resins, oils, and pigments, all of the recipe's ingredients, are indeed given to the community *by God*. But the warmth and wisdom necessary to bind it all together as an oil varnish is the love that is required *of us*."[13] When the church of Christ displays this lustrous love, the world experiences the beauty of our Savior.

The Beautiful Bride

One day, the church—finally—will look as beautiful as her Savior does. The promise of our coming beauty is as ancient as the people of God. Speaking through the prophet Isaiah, God swore to his people, "I will beautify my beautiful house" (Isa. 60:7; cf. Ps. 96:6; Isa. 64:11). That true promise was fulfilled among the Old Testament people of God at the temple in Jerusalem (see Ezek. 16:13–14), and it will be fulfilled again in God's church, which is "the temple of the living God" (2 Cor. 6:16). God wants his Son to be seen in his beauty, and for that reason he also intends for us to become beautiful.

What makes the church beautiful is the loving, living presence of Jesus Christ, our beautiful Savior. Contemporary theologian James

12 Schleske, *Life's Unspeakable Beauty*, 70.
13 Schleske, *Life's Unspeakable Beauty*, 296.

Edwards rightly states, "Apart from the person of Christ, the church has no existence; apart from the message of Christ, the church has no proclamation; apart from the call of Christ, the church has no mission."[14] To further emphasize how important Jesus is to us, we can add this phrase to what Edwards wrote: "Apart from the presence of Christ, the church has no beauty." When Jesus is present in our Christian community, then we practice the hospitality, show the generosity, do the justice, pursue the reconciliation, and display the unity that only his Spirit can create.

Today we face a strong temptation to give up on the church—to watch from home, sit in the back, sleep in, or stop going altogether. Sometimes, in its ugliness, the church has become for us the scene of the crime. Nevertheless, God has promised to beautify his blood-bought bride. This promise is not only as old as God's people but also as eternal as the new heavens and the new earth. Jesus died on the cross specifically because he loved the church and wanted her to appear "in splendor, without spot or wrinkle or any such thing, that she might be holy and without blemish" (Eph. 5:27; cf. Isa. 61:10), like a bride on her wedding day. Simply put, God the Son wants to see in us a beautiful bride.

For his part, Jesus wants people to see his beautiful bride across the whole wide world. This is one way to think about the missionary calling of the church to proclaim the gospel everywhere to everyone: global evangelism is the Spirit's way of making the bride of Christ more beautiful. There is unique splendor in the distinctive beauties of African, Asian, and American Christianity. Indigenous peoples in Australia and across the Pacific Islands lift

14 James Edwards, "A Confessional Church in a Pluralistic Age," Spring 1992 Wheaton Theology Conference.

up songs of praise to the triune God that are utterly original in their rhythms and melodies. The long history of European Christianity makes irreplaceable contributions to our understanding of liturgy and theology. South and Central America have uniquely dynamic patterns of congregational life. The same is true of Christianity in the Middle East and every other place in the world where Christ is already known or is yet to be honored. Pursuing the full diversity of the body of Christ is not a grudging concession to something politically correct or socially demanded but a passionate quest for eternal beauty. Until we get a fully global view of the church, the face of Christ's bride will remain partially veiled.

Is anything more beautiful than a bride on her wedding day? As a minister, I have stood many times at the front of a church, close to the teary-eyed groom as he reaches to take the fair hand of his beloved bride. At every wedding I catch a glimpse of eternal love and infinite beauty. Then I am reminded not to give up on the church, which one day certainly will become as beautiful as the glory of God.

The night before my eldest daughter's wedding, she and her bridesmaids stayed at the home of neighbors who were away on vacation. On the morning of her wedding day—after all their preparations—the house was in disarray. Dirty clothes were draped over the furniture. Curling irons littered the countertops. Rose petals and scraps of ribbon were strewn across the floor. Apparently, it was a mess worth making because when I looked at my daughter in her wedding dress, I could see in her an image of eternal beauty.

Although, admittedly, the analogy has its shortcomings, life in Christ's church also gets messy sometimes, but it too is a mess worth making. God's beautiful Spirit is at work in our community. Our calling is not simply to wait for the beauty that God has promised one day to reveal in the church, his beloved bride. Our calling is to live with a view toward our destined beauty, so that the world can see and know the Savior today.

But Jesus said, "Leave her alone. Why do you trouble
her? She has done a beautiful thing to me."

MARK 14:6

Life's unspeakable beauty is found in this interplay.
Heaven's grace longs to play our faith as a musician
plays her instrument. Indeed, "faith" means placing
yourself in the hands of grace and allowing "music" to
be played through you. Unspeakable beauty emerges
when the bow touches the vibrating string.

MARTIN SCHLESKE

9

It's a Beautiful Life

The Beauty of Generous Living

IN THESE ANXIOUS, TROUBLED TIMES, we are and we ought to be sick of disease, frustrated by political polarization, discouraged by racial division, alarmed by armed conflict, grieved over abortion, scandalized by sex trafficking, burdened for lost souls, and disheartened by the moral downfalls of the church.

In our distress, we can relate to the closing lines of G. K. Chesterton's "The Mortal Answers." As he surveyed the woes of fallen humanity, Chesterton wrote, "The world is hot and cruel, / We are weary of heart and hand." Yet the poet still believed in the beauty of God's redeeming grace. Determined to strengthen tired hands and inspire weary hearts, he wrote that this weary world is also "more full of glory / Than you can understand."[1]

---

1   G. K. Chesterton, *Poems* (London: Burns & Oates, 1915), 44–45.

God has a purpose for this world—and for every one of his servants—that goes beyond everything that is sick and tired, wounded and broken. Without denying the painful realities of sin and death, we believe that God has the power to make all things new. Through the cross and through the empty tomb, our crucified, risen, and now ascended Savior has begun to give us a kingdom.

Throughout this book we have taken a hard look at the ugliness around us—the depravity, division, and degradation—and at the same time tried to see the eternal beauty that God wants to create in us. By the power of the same Holy Spirit who raised Jesus from the dead to immortal splendor, beauty is our destiny. With this goal in mind, we are called to live a beautiful life—what the prophet Jeremiah described as a life "beautiful with good fruit" (Jer. 11:16).

The Woman with the Alabaster Flask

A stunning example of living beautifully for Jesus came near the end of our Lord's earthly ministry, shortly before he was crucified, died, and was buried.

It happened in a little town outside Jerusalem called Bethany, where Jesus of Nazareth had a close circle of friends. It was time to share a meal, and according to the custom of the day, Jesus "was reclining at table" (Mark 14:3). Suddenly, a woman stepped forward to anoint him with sweet perfume. She broke her precious alabaster flask and poured the entire contents on his sacred head. No one who was there that day ever forgot the sight or the smell of perfume running down our Savior's hair, dripping onto his beard, crowning him with the scent of glory.

We know this act was beautiful because Jesus said so. In fact, he gave the woman with the alabaster flask one of the highest compliments he ever gave anyone: "She has done a beautiful thing to me" (Mark 14:6). The better we understand why Jesus said this, the more closely we will be able to follow her example and do something beautiful for Jesus with our lives too.

What the woman did was *simple*. Apparently, we do not have to do anything complicated to do something beautiful. It took only a moment. All she did was break open a flask of ointment and pour it out for Jesus.

What the woman did was *extravagant*. She carried her perfume in an alabaster flask—itself an object of beauty. Mark tells us that the perfume was "pure nard," which is an herbal incense extracted from the spikenard plant. Members of the dinner party did some quick calculations and estimated its market value at "three hundred denarii" (Mark 14:5). This amount would correspond to a full year's wages for a common laborer, or about $40,000 in the current economy—roughly what the same amount of expensive perfume would cost today.

By way of contemporary comparison, the following advertisement describes what it takes Baccarat to produce one of their limited-edition fragrances:

> During two short weeks in summer, several kilos of blossoms are harvested from the Jean Patou flower fields in Grasse to achieve the 10,600 flowers required for just one bottle of Joy perfume. A floral bouquet of Bulgarian rose, Ylang-Ylang, Tuberose and Grasse Jasmine, the scent is a timeless masterpiece in simplicity.[2]

2   "We Ranked 15 Most Expensive Perfumes in the World," Alux, accessed December 20, 2022, https://www.alux.com/.

As of this writing, a single ounce of Baccarat's "timeless master-piece" is on offer for the low, low price of $2,000, which is more or less equivalent to what pure nard cost in biblical times. To pour out an entire flask was to spend a small fortune.

We can also say, therefore, that what the woman did was *sacrificial*. With overflowing love, she gave away something she could never regain. The moment the perfume ran out of her flask, it was gone forever. Only the aroma would linger, and soon it too would be nothing more than a sweet memory. What the woman offered required a sacrifice, therefore, as beauty usually does. Beauty's high cost helps explain why it is rarer than it ought to be, for as the Christian philosopher Roger Scruton has observed, "Beauty is vanishing from our world because we live as though it did not matter; and we live that way because we have lost the habit of sacrifice and are striving always to avoid it."[3]

The woman with the alabaster flask's simple, extravagant sacrifice was also *memorable*—so memorable that we are still talking about it today. A small dinner party, which took place in a poor village over two thousand years ago, turned out to be one of the most famous meals in history. Jesus declared, "Truly, I say to you, wherever the gospel is proclaimed in the whole world, what she has done will be told in memory of her" (Mark 14:9). The poet John Keats must have been right, therefore, when he claimed, "A thing of beauty is a joy for ever."[4] Certainly, this famous aphorism is true of what happened in Bethany. Whenever we call this incident to mind, we

---

3   Roger Scruton, *Beauty: A Very Short Introduction* (Oxford: Oxford University Press, 2011), 161.

4   This is the opening line of Keats's masterpiece *Endymion: A Poetic Romance* (London: Taylor and Hessey, 1818). Public domain.

fulfill the prophecy of Jesus once again and honor the woman who poured out her perfume, as well as the Savior she loved so much that she wanted to do something beautiful in his honor.

The World Needs This Beauty

This true story compels us to do something beautiful for Jesus too—something *he* would say is truly beautiful. It also helps us believe that this is possible. Even something simple can be beautiful and memorable if it is truly done for the honor and glory of Jesus Christ.

Beauty is always meant to be shared. As soon as we see something truly beautiful—a sunset, for example, or an artistic masterpiece—our first impulse is to share it. Immediately, we tell someone else to look at what we are seeing too, or else we take a picture and send it to them. To give an everyday example, I walked into the lobby of a concert hall just as a storm was ending, the sun was starting to shine again, and a beautiful rainbow arced across the sky. Opening the door, I said, "There's a rainbow!" and people rushed outside to take pictures and post them for the enjoyment of others.

Human beings have an irresistible impulse to copy, share, repeat, imitate, and reproduce beautiful things. This is one of the clearest signs that we were made for beauty. As we noted in chapter 1, Elaine Scarry believes that "beauty brings copies of itself into being. It makes us draw it, take photographs of it, or describe it to other people." The experience we have in the presence of something beautiful "seems to incite, even to require, the act of replication."[5] In

---

5 Elaine Scarry, *On Beauty and Being Just* (Princeton, NJ: Princeton University Press, 1999), 3.

response to seeing beauty, she concludes, the beholder often seeks to bring "new beauty into the world."[6] Junius Johnson makes the same point more simply yet equally profoundly: "Beauty aims at the reproduction of another beauty like itself in another."[7]

This is precisely why Mark included the story of the woman with the alabaster flask in his Gospel: he wanted us to break open, pour out, repeat. Here is a beautiful thing—what one woman did with her sweet perfume. Now that we have seen this extravagant act of sacrificial beauty, the evangelist invites us to consider what simple things *we* will do to live a beautiful life.

The world needs beauty now more than ever—beauty that touches the heart of who we are. People who are suffering and grieving need this beauty—those who have been hurt or feel lonely or have lost their loved ones. We still live in the harsh world that Shakespeare described, where "each new morn / New widows howl, new orphans cry, new sorrows / Strike heaven on the face that it resounds."[8] What beauty will it take to wipe away the tears of widows and orphans to give them the healing hope of a new and glorious day?

Junius Johnson argues that most people believe deep down that "the world is not in fact pure ugliness but is shot through with pockets of beauty, radiant havens that push back the inky blackness and give us strength to press forward, to carry on, to dare to hope that all may yet be well." It is on "these moments of

---

6 Scarry, *On Beauty and Being Just*, 88.

7 Junius Johnson, *The Father of Lights: A Theology of Beauty*, Theology for the Life of the World (Grand Rapids, MI: Baker Academic, 2020), 193.

8 William Shakespeare, *Macbeth*, in *The Norton Shakespeare, Based on the Oxford Edition: Tragedies*, ed. Stephen Greenblatt, 2nd ed. (New York: Norton, 2008), act 4, scene 3, lines 4–6.

beauty," as Johnson calls them, that "all hopes of humanity are built: we believe that we can extend them, expand them, and, by so doing, gradually push back the power of darkness until no ugliness remains and we enter the beautiful light."[9] Jesus alone makes this hope viable, and he works this hope into the world through people whose lives have been transformed by his beauty.

We need to see beauty because sometimes all the ugliness makes it hard for us to see God. Philip Yancey writes about this spiritual struggle in his extraordinary memoir, *Where the Light Fell*. With unflinching honesty, Yancey recounts the dark secrets of his childhood, in which death, poverty, hypocrisy, and the thin walls of his mother's trailer home threatened to keep him from seeing the Savior. Yet the beauty came through. It touched his life through classical music and romantic love. It resounded in the fields and forests where Yancey loved to walk alone. Although nature could not save his soul, it did awaken his desire, he testifies, "to meet whoever is responsible for the monarch butterfly."[10]

People often talk about "the problem of evil" as a counterargument to the goodness of God. But what about "the problem of beauty" for anyone who doubts his very existence? Sooner or later, humanity's unavoidable experience of splendor compels most people to consider where the beauty came from. Knowing that this question lingers should compel every Christian to ask, "How can my life replicate God's glory?" If the Russian novelist Fyodor Dostoevsky was right to describe beauty as a mystery in which "God and the devil are fighting and the battlefield is the

9 Johnson, *Father of Lights*, 9.
10 Philip Yancey, *Where the Light Fell: A Memoir* (New York: Convergent, 2021), 236.

heart of man,"[11] then part of our calling is to contest for human souls by bringing more of God's beauty into the world.

Do What You Can!

To answer God's call to live a beautiful life, we do not have to change the world. As we learn from the woman with the alabaster flask, even something as simple as dinner with friends can become a memorable occasion for sacrificial beauty. What Jesus said to her is a massive encouragement to us. When people started to criticize the woman for wasting perfectly good perfume, Jesus not only told them to leave her alone, but he also defended her by saying, "She has done what she could" (Mark 14:8). This is our Savior's standard: not what someone else can do but what *we* can do. So we should do what we can!

We can live a beautiful life by what we create with our hands as an offering of our hearts. This is God's special calling for artists. To cite one example, when the renowned luthier Antonio Stradivari inscribed his initials inside his magnificent violins, he placed them under the sign of a cross.[12] This was Antonio's way of making stringed instruments for the glory of God. Thankfully, we do not have to make a Stradivarius to become what J. R. R. Tolkien called a "sub-creator."[13] As people made in the image of a Maker, all of us have the capacity to create. Even in the simple

11 Fyodor Dostoevsky, *The Brothers Karamazov: A Revised Translation, Contexts, Criticism*, trans. and ed. Susan McReynolds Oddo, Norton Critical Edition (New York: Norton, 2011), 98.

12 Martin Schleske, *The Sound of Life's Unspeakable Beauty*, trans. Janet Gesme (Grand Rapids, MI: Eerdmans, 2020), 261.

13 J. R. R. Tolkien, "On Fairy-Stories," *The Tolkien Reader* (New York: Ballantine, 1966), 3–84.

act of fashioning a home—wherever God calls us—we can create a space more beautiful and therefore more hospitable as a way of showing and telling the beauty of God.

We live a beautiful life by the music we make—especially when we share it as a gift for others, in Jesus's name. Yancey also writes about this in his memoir. He was never as gifted as his older brother, who was a musical genius. But when Yancey nervously played the piano for his girlfriend on her birthday, he offered a simple gift that brought them both to tears.[14] When it comes to music, trained musicians may have the most to give. But every one of us has been blessed with a voice for praise, located in a body that happens to be the most resonant, versatile musical instrument ever designed. All of us can make at least some music for Jesus.

We live a beautiful life by joining the broken yet beautiful community that God calls "the church." Together, we are "the embodied presence of Christ in the world,"[15] and therefore we are called to display our Savior's beauty. What we do together—in worship, ministry, outreach, and evangelism—can and ought to be more beautiful than what we do alone.

We live a beautiful life by seeking the *shalom* of our community—its total well-being. Joel Hamernick—who leads Sunshine Gospel Ministries in Chicago's Woodlawn neighborhood—stressed the importance of pursuing God's peace in one of his ministry news-letters. *Shalom* is not possible, he argued, in any place that is "void of beauty"; instead, he asserted,

---

14 Yancey, *Where the Light Fell*, 241.
15 W. David O. Taylor, *The Theater of God's Glory: Calvin, Creation, and the Liturgical Arts* (Grand Rapids, MI: Eerdmans, 2017), 131.

I see communities like ours as exhibiting beauty that is unrecognized (and therefore should be identified and celebrated) and under-valued through the development of buildings, blocks, lighting, that lack creativity and fail to inspire joy—for example, every window blocked by metal bars, ordering your food through a bullet-proof, scratched up, Plexi-glass window, or sitting in an ugly, barren public service office for assistance (where you often have to sit for hours to get anything done).

Part of Hamernick's recipe for *shalom* is a commitment to simple beauty in everyday life. Cities like Chicago—with the millions of people who live there, each one made in the image of God—ought to be some of the most beautiful places in the world. Where they are broken, therefore, "we need to provide more beautiful things and surroundings for those who live and work nearby as a means of improving the public good."[16] Cleaning streets, planting window boxes, turning abandoned lots into small parks, designing and executing mural art—these simple acts of beauty make a tangible difference to community life. The people who do them are like the woman with the alabaster flask: they live with the beauty of Jesus.

We live a beautiful life by doing justice, which is also part of what it takes to make our neighborhoods more beautiful. Because it demeans and diminishes people made in the image of God, injustice is always ugly. Indeed, "a world in which there is not justice is a world without beauty."[17] Sometimes fighting for

16 Nancy Perkins Spyke, "The Instrumental Value of Beauty in the Pursuit of Justice," *University of San Francisco Law Review* 40, no. 2 (2006): 452.
17 Johnson, *Father of Lights*, 37.

justice can be ugly too, if it is done with unrighteous anger. But the loving pursuit of justice brings more beauty into the world. Yancey spoke about this in one of his interviews. Acknowledging that when Christians pursue political power, they fail to gain a positive reputation, Yancey talked about what he witnessed in the ninety countries where he traveled to share the gospel: "Wherever I go, where Christians have been—missionaries—you see a string of orphanages and clinics and hospitals and education places and people fighting sexual trafficking and digging wells and feeding the hungry." When people in those places define what a Christian is, they say, "It's somebody who when I'm sick they make me well and when I'm hungry they give me food."[18] Beautiful!

We live a beautiful life by spending more of our money for the kingdom. Generous giving is one of the simplest ways to make a beautiful sacrifice. Therefore, we should give more than we think we can spare to sustain the gospel witness of our local church, to care for the poor, to sustain effective Christian organizations, and to support brothers and sisters who are called to missionary service.

Brandon Chasteen promotes extravagant generosity in a thoughtful poem about paying his son five dollars to rake a pile of leaves. Sensing a teachable moment on the value of steward-ship, he advised his son to spend one dollar, tithe another, and save the other three. Chasteen was caught short by his son's response, which caused him to repent for being so stingy. His sonnet ends,

---

18 Philip Yancey and Adam Weber, "Philip Yancey on *Where the Light Fell*," October 6, 2021, episode 134 in *The Conversation with Andy Weber*, podcast, 24:14, https://www.adamweber.com/.

May God forgive
What scorn I showed to him, when saying there
Were reasons, he supposed, for giving
All his earning to our church.[19]

When we give as much as we can to the kingdom, we get a beautiful return on our investment.

We live a beautiful life by caring for creation, which is a way of preserving one of our Father's greatest masterpieces. As a leading evangelical, the English theologian John Stott came more and more to see creation care as an important aspect of Christian witness. In his farewell to the worldwide church, Stott listed "the care of our created environment" as essential to Christian discipleship and integral to fulfilling the Great Commission.[20] So plant trees, tend gardens, clean up local parks, live sustainably. Follow the example of Samwise Gamgee. At the end of all his adventures in Tolkien's *The Lord of the Rings*, Sam returned home to the Shire and planted "saplings in all the places where specially beautiful and beloved trees had been destroyed."[21]

My own desire to care for creation has been heightened by my personal experience with changing natural habitats. As an amateur (but enthusiastic) ornithologist, I have watched native bird populations dwindle in North America over the last half century. I have also had the extraordinary privilege of traveling to

---

19 Brandon Chasteen, "Christmas Sonnet," *First Things*, January 2021. Used by permission of the author.

20 John Stott, *Radical Disciple: Some Neglected Aspects of Our Calling* (London: Inter-Varsity Press, 2014), 49.

21 J. R. R. Tolkien, *The Lord of the Rings*, part 3, *The Return of the King* (New York: Houghton Mifflin, 1993), 1035.

Antarctica, where I hiked on icy mountains, sailed through seas of massive icebergs, and gazed in wonder as mighty whales coursed through frigid waters and feasted on an abundance of tiny krill. The unique beauty of the frozen continent remains undiminished. Yet I also experienced signs of coming danger: unseasonably warm temperatures, receding glaciers, and the shocking accumulation of microplastics in earth's polar regions. How will the people of God care for the world that our Savior created and came to redeem?

Never forget that preaching the gospel is beautiful too. In fact, the prophet Isaiah said that even the *feet* of someone who proclaims good news are beautiful (see Isa. 52:7; Rom. 10:15). The result is even more beautiful: hearts are changed, lives are transformed, and heaven rejoices. One international student described the moment when Jesus came into her life. She honored the host who had welcomed her to the United States by saying, "You built a bridge to me—a bridge of friendship. Then one day Jesus came walking over the bridge." Beautiful!

There are so many ways to live a beautiful life. If beauty is the visible glory of God, then we should make whatever life sacrifices it takes for others to see his beauty alongside us.

Beauty by Sacrifice

Where do we learn how to live such a beautiful life? From the beautiful life that Jesus lived and the beautiful death he died.

Mark artfully frames the story of the dinner party in Bethany between two editorial comments that advance his gospel plot. He opens chapter 14 by informing us that "the chief priests and the scribes" were keeping their eye on Jesus and "seeking how to arrest him by stealth and kill him" (Mark 14:1). With these ominous words, a dark shadow falls across the page. Jesus has enemies who want to kill him. Then in Mark 14:10 the story takes an even more sinister turn as Judas goes "to the chief priests in order to betray him." Something terrible is about to happen, for Judas has made a deadly bargain to sell out the Savior of the world.

It is specifically in this context—of a coming crucifixion—that the woman with the alabaster flask goes "all in" and pours out her perfume. Jesus recognizes this gesture for what it is: a symbol of his embalming. He says, "She has anointed my body beforehand for burial" (Mark 14:8). Because of the dark frame that Mark has set around the narrative, this line stands out on the biblical page. It declares that the woman's costly sacrifice was emblematic of the even more costly sacrifice that Jesus was ready to make for her by dying on the cross for her sins.

In one sense, the crucifixion was simple: all it took was for Jesus to offer one atonement to God. At the same time, it was infinitely extravagant: Jesus poured out his perfectly precious lifeblood as the Son of God. This sacrifice was so memorable that Jesus gets praised for it every moment of every day, all around the world. In a word, the simple, extravagant, memorable, sacrificial cross was beautiful!

What blossomed on dark Golgotha was the costly, beautiful sacrifice that saved the world. Now anyone saved by this sacrifice is called to reproduce its beauty. Indeed, as Belden Lane has written, "the replication of God's beauty in human life" is only complete when "the beauty is shared with others."[22] This is how the world will see its Savior: in the cross-shaped lives that we lay down for others.

22 Belden C. Lane, *Ravished by Beauty: The Surprising Legacy of Reformed Spirituality* (Oxford: Oxford University Press, 2011), 194.

When people see in us the good news of God's love, we point them toward eternity. Their new experience of beauty awakens in them a deep longing that can be satisfied only by believing in a beautiful Savior. Even if they do not know fully how to express it, they want to see his beauty re-created in their lives. Like C. S. Lewis, they are haunted by "the scent of a flower we have not found, the echo of a tune we have not heard, news from a country we have never yet visited,"[23] and they confess, "The sweetest thing in all my life has been the longing . . . to find the place where all the beauty came from."[24] And not just to find it but also to join it. As Lewis also wrote,

> We do not want merely to *see* beauty, though, God knows, even that is bounty enough. We want something else which can hardly be put into words—to be united with the beauty we see, to pass into it, to receive it into ourselves, to bathe in it, to become part of it.[25]

When the early church father Gregory of Nyssa experienced the same ineffable longing, he turned it into a prayer for grace. "The ardent lover of beauty," he wrote, "longs to be filled with the very stamp of the archetype. And the bold request which goes up the mountains of desire asks this: to enjoy the Beauty not in mirrors and reflections, but face to face."[26]

---

23 C. S. Lewis, "The Weight of Glory," in *The Weight of Glory and Other Addresses*, ed. Walter Hooper, rev. ed. (New York: Macmillan, 1980), 7.

24 C. S. Lewis, *Till We Have Faces* (London: Geoffrey Bles, 1956), 83.

25 Lewis, "Weight of Glory," 16.

26 Gregory of Nyssa, quoted in Patrick Sherry, *Spirit and Beauty: An Introduction to Theological Aesthetics*, 2nd ed. (London: SCM, 2002), 56.

Our hunger for this beatific vision is infinite. We never get enough of it. If we see something beautiful, we want to experience it again. And such insatiable desire can be satisfied only in the face of our Savior.

Thankfully, as "the pre-appearance of the coming truth,"[27] our experience of earthly beauty shows us our destiny. God has promised through faith in Christ one day to raise us up in immortal splendor and to make us as beautiful as his own beloved Son. Isaiah describes God's holy majesty as "a crown of glory, / and a diadem of beauty" (Isa. 28:5). Later, the prophet uses the same words to describe the people that the coming Savior will redeem:

You shall be a crown of beauty in the hand of the LORD,
    and a royal diadem in the hand of your God. (Isa. 62:3)

The Savior is a glorious crown, and we are God's crowning glory, which is Isaiah's way of saying that we are destined to become the beauty that we behold in Jesus.

This beautiful transformation will take place on the day of our glorification with the risen and ascended Christ, when God "will transform our lowly body to be like his glorious body" (Phil. 3:21). The entire cosmos will be renewed and re-created as a new heaven and a new earth. And in "the glittering finale of a world remade,"[28]

27 Eberhard Jüngel, "Even the Beautiful Must Die," quoted in Jeremy S. Begbie, "Created Beauty: The Witness of J. S. Bach," in *The Beauty of God: Theology and the Arts*, ed. Daniel J. Treier, Mark Husbands, and Roger Lundin (Downers Grove, IL: IVP Academic, 2007), 28.

28 Jeremy S. Begbie, *The Art of New Creation*, quoted in Matthew J. Milliner, "Makoto Fujimura and the Art of New Creation," *Marginalia*, May 6, 2022, https://the marginaliareview.com/.

where God will dwell with us and be our God (Rev. 21:1–3), we will find our eternal home.

That great day is coming sooner than we know. In the meantime—when beauty seems to vanish from the world and there is more ugliness than we can bear—we are called to do what we can, no matter the cost, to live a beautiful life for Jesus.

General Index

Scripture Index

Also Available from Philip Ryken

For more information, visit **crossway.org**.